Your All-in-One Resource

On the CD that accompanies this book, you'll find additional resources to enhance your learning.

The reference library includes the following fully searchable titles:

- *Microsoft Computer Dictionary*, 5th ed.
- *First Look 2007 Microsoft Office System* by Katherine Murray
- Windows Vista Product Guide

Also provided are a sample chapter and poster from *Look Both Ways: Help Protect Your Family on the Internet* by Linda Criddle.

The CD interface has a new look. You can use the tabs for an assortment of tasks:

- Check for book updates (if you have Internet access)
- Install the book's practice file
- Go online for product support or CD support
- Send us feedback

The following screen shot gives you a glimpse of the new interface.

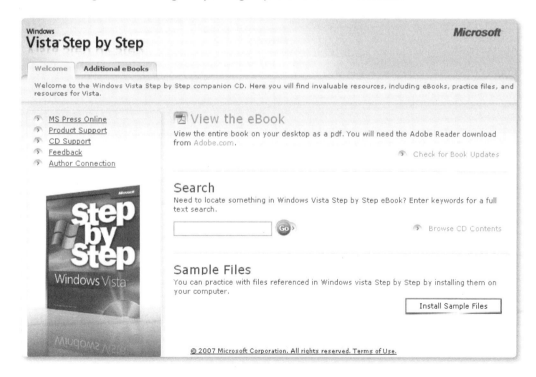

Microsoft

Microsoft®
Expression® Web
Step by Step

Chris Leeds

PUBLISHED BY
Microsoft Press
A Division of Microsoft Corporation
One Microsoft Way
Redmond, Washington 98052-6399

Copyright © 2008 by Chris Leeds

Library of Congress Control Number: 2007934741

Printed and bound in the United States of America.

1 2 3 4 5 6 7 8 9   QWT   2 1 0 9 8 7

Distributed in Canada by H.B. Fenn and Company Ltd.

A CIP catalogue record for this book is available from the British Library.

Microsoft Press books are available through booksellers and distributors worldwide. For further information about international editions, contact your local Microsoft Corporation office or contact Microsoft Press International directly at fax (425) 936-7329. Visit our Web site at www.microsoft.com/mspress. Send comments to mspinput@microsoft.com.

Microsoft, Expression, Fluent, Front Page, Internet Explorer, Microsoft Press, Outlook, Visual Basic, Visual Web Developer, Windows, Windows Server, and Windows Vista are either registered trademarks or trademarks of Microsoft Corporation in the United States and/or other countries. Other product and company names mentioned herein may be the trademarks of their respective owners.

The example companies, organizations, products, domain names, e-mail addresses, logos, people, places, and events depicted herein are fictitious. No association with any real company, organization, product, domain name, e-mail address, logo, person, place, or event is intended or should be inferred.

This book expresses the author's views and opinions. The information contained in this book is provided without any express, statutory, or implied warranties. Neither the authors, Microsoft Corporation, nor its resellers, or distributors will be held liable for any damages caused or alleged to be caused either directly or indirectly by this book.

Acquisitions Editor: Juliana Aldous Atkinson
Developmental Editor: Sandra Haynes
Project Editor: Kathleen Atkins
Editorial Production: Online Training Solutions, Inc.
Technical Reviewer: Derek Lakin; Technical Review services provided by Content Master, a member of CM Group, Ltd.

Body Part No. X14-16811

Contents

What do you think of this book? We want to hear from you!

Microsoft is interested in hearing your feedback so we can continually improve our books and learning resources for you. To participate in a brief online survey, please visit:

www.microsoft.com/learning/booksurvey/

Introducing Expression Web

Microsoft Expression Web is the newest Web editing and management application from Microsoft. It is a professional design tool used to create modern, standards-based sites that deliver superior quality on the Web. Expression Web also holds the distinction of being the replacement for Microsoft Office FrontPage, a long-lived and very popular Web editing and management tool.

Expression Web can be purchased alone or as part of Microsoft Expression Studio, which is an integrated group of applications that, besides Expression Web, includes the following:

- **Expression Blend.** A professional design tool used to create engaging, Web-connected multimedia experiences for Windows.

- **Expression Design.** A professional illustration and graphic design tool used for building compelling elements for both Web and desktop application user interfaces.

- **Expression Media.** A professional asset management tool for visually cataloging and organizing all your digital assets, and that provides for effortless retrieval and presentation.

From the perspective of a designer or developer, the modern Web bears only a slight resemblance to the Web of as little as five years ago. Expression Web is an effort by Microsoft to provide a tool that helps designers attain modern Web design standards and practices to a large group of designers.

Expression Web includes features that help ensure your output keeps within the World Wide Web Consortium (W3C) validity standards, and that enable you to cleanly separate content from presentation by taking advantage of the functionality and capabilities in cascading style sheets.

As you drill deeper into Expression Web, you will find tools to make working with Microsoft ASP.NET much more comfortable than ever before, such as the ASP.NET Development Server that installs with Expression Web and the ASP.NET Controls group in the Toolbox task pane.

Expression Web helps you easily use some of the new features in ASP.NET 2.0, which are just the ticket for designers interested in validity, accessibility, and a best practices type of workflow. Specifically, ASP.NET Master Pages, Navigation Controls, and Data Controls spring to mind. It's refreshing that tools with this type of power are available in a user-friendly "designer's" application like Expression Web as opposed to being relegated to a very "programmer-oriented" tool such as Microsoft Visual Web Developer or Microsoft Visual Studio.

Upgrading from FrontPage

Former FrontPage devotees may be dismayed at first glance to find many of the familiar "Web Bots" and components are not present in Expression Web. Not to worry. Firstly, even if you install Expression Web as an upgrade to FrontPage, you will still be able to retain the FrontPage application on your system, so you can always use FrontPage with your previous work that relied heavily on FrontPage features. Secondly, everything that was in FrontPage that didn't make its way into Expression Web stayed behind for a reason. The feature either wrote W3C-invalid code, relied on browser-specific rendering, required proprietary server software, or suffered a combination of those shortcomings.

You should feel comfortable using your existing copy of FrontPage to maintain previous work that relies on its proprietary features, but be sure to move forward with Expression Web by creating and maintaining your new work with it; the program provides too many benefits not to.

Information for Readers Running Windows XP

The graphics and the operating system–related instructions in this book reflect the Windows Vista user interface, but you can also use a computer running Windows XP with Service Pack 2 (SP2) installed.

Most of the differences you will encounter when working through the exercises in this book on a computer running Windows XP relate to appearance rather than functionality. For example, the Windows Vista Start button is round rather than rectangular and is not labeled with the word *Start*; window frames and window-management buttons look different; and if your system supports Windows Aero, the window frames might be transparent. In addition, file system dialog boxes and some file system paths are different between the two platforms. For example, the *My Documents* folder in Windows XP is named *Documents* in Windows Vista.

In this section, we provide steps for navigating to or through menus and dialog boxes in Windows XP that differ from those provided in the exercises in this book. For the most part, these differences are small enough that you will have no difficulty in completing the exercises.

Managing the Practice Files

The instructions given in the "Using the Book's CD" section are specific to Windows Vista. The only differences when installing, using, uninstalling, and removing the practice files supplied on the companion CD are the default installation location and the uninstall process.

On a computer running Windows Vista, the default installation location of the practice files is *Documents\Microsoft Press\Expression Web SBS*. On a computer running Windows XP, the default installation location is *My Documents\ Microsoft Press\Expression Web SBS*. If your computer is running Windows XP, whenever an exercise tells you to navigate to your *Documents* folder, you should instead go to your *My Documents* folder.

To uninstall the practice files from a computer running Windows XP:

1. On the Windows taskbar, click the **Start** button, and then click **Control Panel**.
2. In **Control Panel**, click (or in Classic view, double-click) **Add or Remove Programs**.
3. In the **Add or Remove Programs** window, click **Microsoft Expression Web Step by Step**, and then click **Remove**.
4. In the **Add or Remove Programs** message box asking you to confirm the deletion, click **Yes**.

> **Important** If you need help installing or uninstalling the practice files, please see the "Getting Help" section later in this book. Microsoft Product Support Services does not provide support for this book or its companion CD.

Using the Start Menu

Folders on the Windows Vista Start menu expand vertically. Folders on the Windows XP Start menu expand horizontally. However, the steps to access a command on the Start menu are identical on both systems.

To start Microsoft Expression Web on a Windows XP computer:

→ Click the **Start** button, point to **All Programs**, click **Microsoft Expression**, and then click **Microsoft Expression Web**.

Navigating Dialog Boxes

On a computer running Windows XP, some of the dialog boxes you will work with in the exercises not only look different from the graphics shown in this book but also work differently. These dialog boxes are primarily those that act as an interface between Expression Web and the operating system, including any dialog box in which you navigate to a specific location.

For example, to navigate to the *My Pictures* folder in Windows XP:

→ On the **Places** bar, click **My Documents**. Then in the folder content pane, double-click **My Pictures**.

To move back to the *My Documents* folder in Windows XP:

Up One Level

→ On the toolbar, click the **Up One Level** button.

Features and Conventions of This Book

This book has been designed to lead you step by step through all the tasks you are most likely to want to perform in Microsoft Expression Web. If you start at the beginning and work your way through all the exercises, you will gain enough proficiency to be able to create complex Web sites and pages. However, each topic is self contained. If you have worked with another Web editor, such as Microsoft Office FrontPage, or if you completed all the exercises and later need help remembering how to perform a procedure, the following features of this book will help you locate specific information:

● **Detailed table of contents.** Scan this listing of the topics and sidebars within each chapter to quickly find the information you want.

● **Chapter thumb tabs.** Easily locate the beginning of the chapter you want.

● **Topic-specific running heads.** Within a chapter, quickly locate the topic you want by looking at the running head of odd-numbered pages.

● **Detailed index.** Look up specific tasks and features and general concepts in the index, which has been carefully crafted with the reader in mind.

● **Companion CD.** Install the practice files needed for the step-by-step exercises, and consult a fully searchable electronic version of this book and other useful resources contained on this CD.

In addition, we provide a glossary of terms for those times when you need to look up the meaning of a word or the definition of a concept.

You can save time when you use this book by understanding how the *Step by Step* series shows special instructions, keys to press, buttons to click, and so on.

Convention	Meaning
	This icon indicates a reference to the book's companion CD.
USE	This paragraph preceding a step-by-step exercise indicates the practice files or programs that you will use when working through the exercise.
BE SURE TO	This paragraph preceding or following a step-by-step exercise indicates any requirements you should attend to before beginning the exercise or actions you should take to restore your system after completing the exercise.
OPEN	This paragraph preceding a step-by-step exercise indicates files that you should open before beginning the exercise.
CLOSE	This paragraph following a step-by-step exercise provides instructions for closing open files or programs before moving on to another topic.
1 **2**	Large numbered steps guide you through hands-on exercises in each topic.
1 2	Small numbered steps guide you through procedures in sidebars and in expository text.
→	An arrow indicates a procedure that has only one step.
Tip	These paragraphs provide a helpful hint or shortcut that makes working through a task easier, or information about other available options.
Important	These paragraphs point out information that you need to know to complete a procedure.
Troubleshooting	These paragraphs warn you of potential missteps that might prevent you from continuing with the exercise.
See Also	These paragraphs direct you to more information about a given topic in this book or elsewhere.
Enter	In step-by-step exercises, keys you must press appear as they would on a keyboard.
Ctrl + Tab	A plus sign (+) between two key names means that you must hold down the first key while you press the second key. For example, "Press Ctrl + Tab" means "hold down the Ctrl key while you press the Tab key."
Program interface elements and user input	In steps, the names of program elements, such as buttons, commands, and dialog boxes, are shown in bold characters. Text that you are supposed to type is shown in bold characters.
Glossary terms	Terms explained in the glossary are shown in bold italic type.
Paths and emphasized words	Folder paths, URLs, and emphasized words are shown in italic characters.

Using the Book's CD

The companion CD included with this book contains the practice files and sample sites you'll use as you work through the book's exercises, as well as other electronic resources that will help you learn how to use Microsoft Expression Web.

What's on the CD?

The companion CD contains practice files and sample sites necessary to complete the exercises, as well as sample sites depicting the results of completed exercises. The following table lists the practice files and sites supplied on the book's CD.

Chapter	Files and sites
Chapter 1: Understanding How Expression Web Works	Sample Sites\CH1 Sample Sites\Publish\CH1
Chapter 2: Moving From FrontPage to Expression Web	Sample Sites\CH2 Sample Sites\CH2-Done Sample Sites\FrontPageExample Sample Sites\FrontPageExample-Done Files\Microsoft_FrontPage_to_ Expression_Web.doc
Chapter 3: Becoming Familiar with Modern Web Site Standards	Sample Sites\CH3 Sample Sites\CH3-Done
Chapter 4: Presenting Information on a Web Page	Sample Sites\CH4 Sample Site\CH4-Done
Chapter 5: Enhancing a Web Site with Images	Sample Sites\CH5 Samples Sites\CH5-Import Sample Sites\CH5-Done
Chapter 6: Creating Web Sites from a Template	Sample Sites\CH6-Done Files\CH6-images-import
Chapter 7: Creating a Web Site from Scratch	Sample Sites\CH7-Done Files\CH7template Files\Code\CH7CSS.txt

Chapter	Files and sites
Chapter 8: Taking It to the Next Level	*Sample Sites\CH8* *Sample Sites\CH8-Done* *Files\CH8.fwp*
Chapter 9: Publishing a Web Site	*Sample Sites\CH9* *Sample Sites\Publish\CH9*
Chapter 10: Managing a Web Site	*Sample Sites\CH10* *Sample Sites\Publish* *CH10SelectivePublish*
Chapter 11: Using ASP.NET Features	*Sample Sites\CH11* *Sample Sites\CH11-Done*

In addition to the practice files and sample sites, the CD contains some exciting resources that will enhance your ability to get the most out of using this book and Expression Web, including the following:

- *Microsoft Expression Web Step by Step* in eBook format

- *Microsoft Computer Dictionary, 5th ed.* eBook

- *First Look 2007 Microsoft Office System* eBook

- *Microsoft Office Fluent Ribbon Quick Reference*

- *Windows Vista Product Guide*

> **Important** The companion CD for this book does not contain the Expression Web software. You should purchase and install that software before using this book.

Minimum System Requirements

To perform the exercises in this book, your computer should meet the following requirements:

- **Processor.** Pentium 700 megahertz (MHz) or higher; 2 gigahertz (GHz) recommended.

- **Memory.** 512 megabytes (MB) of RAM; 1 gigabyte (GB) or more recommended.

- **Hard disk.** For the eBooks and downloads, we recommend 3 GB of available hard disk space with 2 GB on the hard disk where the operating system is installed.

> **Tip** Hard disk space requirements will vary depending on configuration; custom installation choices might require more or less hard disk space.

- **Operating System.** Windows Vista or later, Windows XP with Service Pack 2 (SP2), or Windows Server 2003 with Service Pack 1 (SP1) or later.
- **Drive.** CD or DVD drive.
- **Display.** Monitor with 1024×768 or higher screen resolution and 16-bit or higher color depth.
- **Software.** Windows Internet Explorer 7 or later or Microsoft Internet Explorer 6 with service packs.

Step-by-Step Exercises

In addition to the hardware, software, and connections required to run Expression Web, you will need the following to successfully complete the exercises in this book:

- Microsoft Expression Web
- 18 MB of available hard disk space for the practice files

Installing the Practice Files

Some exercises in *Microsoft Expression Web Step by Step* use the Web site templates included when you install Expression Web. For other exercises, there are practice files and sample sites that come on this book's accompanying CD.

To install the files from the CD:

1. Remove the companion CD from the envelope at the back of the book, and insert it into the CD drive of your computer.

The Step By Step Companion CD License Terms appear. Follow the on-screen directions. To use the practice files, you must accept the terms of the license agreement. After you accept the license agreement, a menu screen appears.

> **Important** If the menu screen does not appear, click the Start button and then click Computer. Display the Folders list in the Navigation Pane, click the icon for your CD drive, and then in the right pane, double-click the StartCD executable file.

2. Click **Install Practice Files**.

3. Click **Next** on the first screen, and then click **Next** to accept the terms of the license agreement on the next screen.

4. If you want to install the practice files to a location other than the default folder (*Documents\Microsoft Press\Expression Web SBS*), click the **Change** button, select the new drive and path, and then click **OK**.

> **Important** If you install the practice files to a location other than the default, you will need to substitute that path within the exercises.

5. Click **Next** on the **Choose Destination Location** screen, and then click **Install** on the **Ready to Install the Program** screen to install the selected practice files.

6. After the practice files have been installed, click **Finish**.

7. Close the **Step by Step Companion CD** window, remove the companion CD from the CD drive, and return it to the envelope at the back of the book.

Using the Practice Files

When you install the practice files and sample sites from the companion CD, the files are stored on your hard disk in chapter-specific subfolders under *Documents\Microsoft Press\Expression Web SBS*. Each exercise is preceded by a Housekeeping segment that lists the sample Web site needed for that exercise and any extra tasks you need to complete before you start working through the exercise, as shown here:

> **USE** the *CH3* sample site. This site is located in the *Documents\Microsoft Press\Expression Web SBS\Sample Sites* folder.
>
> **BE SURE TO** start Expression Web before beginning this exercise.
>
> **OPEN** the *CH3* site, and display the *default.htm* page in Split view.

Wherever possible, we made the exercises independent of each other. However, if you choose to do exercises in a sequence other than that presented in the book, be aware that there are exercises in some chapters that depend on other exercises performed earlier in the book. If this is the case, we will tell you where in the book the prerequisite exercises are located.

You can browse to the practice files in Windows Explorer by following these steps:

Start

1. On the Windows taskbar, click the **Start** button, and then click **Documents**.

2. In your **Documents** folder, double-click **Microsoft Press**, double-click **Expression Web SBS**, and then double-click a specific chapter folder or site.

Removing the Practice Files

You can free up hard disk space by uninstalling the practice files that were installed from the companion CD. The uninstall process deletes any files that you created in the *Documents\Microsoft Press\Expression Web SBS* folder while working through the exercises.

Follow these steps:

Start

1. On the Windows taskbar, click the **Start** button, and then click **Control Panel**.

2. In **Control Panel**, under **Programs**, click the **Uninstall a program** task.

3. If the **Programs and Features** message box asking you to confirm the deletion appears, click **Yes**.

See Also If you need additional help installing or uninstalling the practice files, see the "Getting Help" section later in this book.

> **Important** Microsoft Product Support Services does not provide support for this book or its companion CD.

Getting Help

Every effort has been made to ensure the accuracy of this book and the contents of its CD. If you run into problems, please contact the appropriate source, listed in the following sections, for help and assistance.

Getting Help with This Book and Its CD

If your question or issue concerns the content of this book or its companion CD, please first search the online Microsoft Press Knowledge Base, which provides support information for known errors in or corrections to this book, at the following Web site:

www.microsoft.com/mspress/support/search.asp/

If you do not find your answer in the online Knowledge Base, send your comments or questions to Microsoft Learning Technical Support at:

mspinput@microsoft.com

Getting Help with Microsoft Expression Web

If your question is about Expression Web, and not about the content of this Microsoft Press book, please search the Microsoft Help and Support Center or the Microsoft Knowledge Base at:

support.microsoft.com

You can also visit the following Web site, where you can ask Chris Leeds, the author of this book, any specific questions you may have about Expression Web and find other Expression Web–related resources.

www.ExpressionWebStepByStep.com

In the United States, Microsoft software product support issues not covered by the Microsoft Knowledge Base are addressed by Microsoft Product Support Services. The Microsoft software support options available from Microsoft Product Support Services are listed at:

www.microsoft.com/services/microsoftservices/srv_support.mspx

Outside the United States, for support information specific to your location, please refer to the Worldwide Support menu on the Microsoft Help And Support Web site for the site specific to your country:

support.microsoft.com/common/international.aspx

Chapter at a Glance

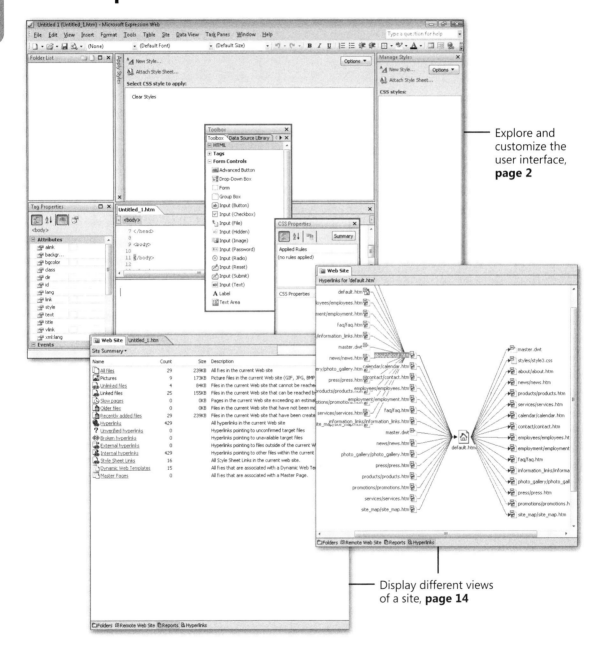

Explore and customize the user interface, **page 2**

Display different views of a site, **page 14**

1 Understanding How Expression Web Works

In this chapter, you will learn to:

- ✔ Explore and customize the user interface.
- ✔ Open an existing site.
- ✔ Display different views of a site.
- ✔ Explore an individual Web page.
- ✔ Understand basic Expression Web concepts.

Microsoft Expression Web is a new program that allows you to easily build *standards-compliant* and *accessible* Web sites. Expression Web also has features that allow you to build components on your site that previously required significant hand coding or a code editing application such as Microsoft Visual Studio or Microsoft Visual Web Developer. Whether you're simply interested in building a standards-based Web site or bringing your existing site up to current standards—that is, to reflect the latest *World Wide Web Consortium (W3C), HTML/XHTML*, and accessibility standards—Expression Web is a great tool to choose. As a bonus, by using Expression Web, you are also creating a Web site that has valid code that is based on *cascading style sheets*.

Basing a site on current W3C standards aids in ease of long-term maintenance, *cross-browser compatibility*, and accessibility by both *search engines* and nonvisual browsers such as *screen readers* that are used by vision-impaired visitors.

Users of Microsoft Office FrontPage will find the transition to Expression Web fairly easy. Though Expression Web ignores most *FrontPage proprietary* features, it allows the full capability of editing and managing sites that were originally created by using FrontPage. The goal for Expression Web is to make the transition to standards-compliant, modern Web sites as painless as possible.

In this chapter, you will explore and customize the *user interface* and open an existing site. You will also use the views in Expression Web to explore an individual Web page. Finally, you will learn some basic Expression Web concepts.

Important Before you can use the practice files in this chapter, you need to install them from the book's companion CD to their default location. See "Using the Book's CD" on page xiii for more information.

Troubleshooting Graphics and operating system–related instructions in this book reflect the Windows Vista user interface. If your computer is running Windows XP and you experience trouble following the instructions as written, please refer to the "Information for Readers Running Windows XP" section at the beginning of this book.

Exploring and Customizing the User Interface

If you're familiar with FrontPage or other Office applications (prior to the 2007 Office system), you will find the user interface in Expression Web to be fairly familiar. Almost everything you might need to do within Expression Web is available to you from the 12 menus on the menu bar. These menus are "intelligent," in that the items you use most often move up the list that appears when you open a menu, and items that you use less frequently are moved down. If an item can't be used, that particular menu item will be unavailable and indicated by a grey color instead of black. In addition to the menu bar and toolbar, Expression Web includes additional panes that are part of your workspace. You can resize, move, *dock*, and *undock* these panes.

Pane   Menu bar   Code pane   Common toolbar   Pane

Pane   Views   Design pane   Status bar   Pane

In this exercise, you will learn to start and exit Expression Web, familiarize yourself with the toolbar commands, and manipulate the panes that are available to you. There are no practice files for this exercise.

 BE SURE TO install Expression Web before beginning this exercise.

1. Click **Start**, point to **All Programs**, point to **Microsoft Expression**, and then click **Expression Web**.

You'll see a page named *Untitled_1.htm* when you start Expression Web for the first time.

> **Troubleshooting** If you previously had a site open with Expression Web, that site will open automatically by default. If that's the case, click Close Site on the File menu, click Exit on the File menu, and then restart Expression Web.

2. On the menu bar, click the **File** menu to reveal its contents.

3. On the **File** menu, point to **New**.

You'll see that you have the ability to create a new page, Web site, HTML or *ASPX* file, or cascading style sheet.

> **Troubleshooting** Notice that the command for creating a new folder is unavailable. You do not have a site open, and folders can be created only within a site.

4. Continue to explore the commands on the **File** menu. Then explore the **Edit**, **View**, **Insert**, **Format**, **Tools**, **Table**, **Site**, **Data View**, **Task Panes**, **Window**, and **Help** menus.

There's a large array of items available on these menus. Don't let them overwhelm you. The point of this exercise is not to learn each and every one of these items but to become familiar with the contents of the menus and to understand the logical groups in which items are arranged.

> **Tip** As you're exploring here, don't forget to also explore the menus that have an arrow so that you can see what is available in that secondary *menu group*.

Below the menu bar, you'll find the Common toolbar. This toolbar contains the most commonly used tools that you'll need when designing pages.

5. Using the mouse pointer, point to each of the buttons on the **Common** toolbar to reveal its *tooltip*.

> **Tip** Toolbar buttons with small downward-pointing arrows indicate that a subgroup is available for that particular button. You'll want to explore these subgroups to become familiar with the available options.

Toolbar Options

6. At the end of the toolbar, you'll see a downward-pointing arrow with a small horizontal line above it. This is the **Toolbar Options** button. Click this button to reveal the option to **Add or Remove Buttons**.

7. Click **Add or Remove Buttons**, and you will see two options: **Common** and **Customize**.

By default all buttons are present on the Common toolbar.

8. Click **Customize** to open the **Customize** dialog box. Explore the three tabs— Toolbars, Commands, and Options—to find out what you can add and remove from the toolbars.

When the Customize dialog box is open, you can move and remove toolbar buttons by dragging them, and you can also enlarge the size of the buttons.

All the toolbars that are available in Expression Web can be dragged over your workspace or docked against any side of the workspace.

9. Drag the **Common** toolbar by the handle on its far left side and drop it in the middle of your workspace.

This is called a "floating" toolbar.

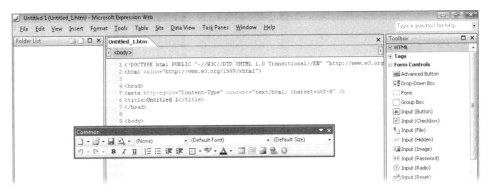

10. Drag the toolbar again, to the right edge of your workspace.

Now the Common toolbar is docked to the right side of your workspace.

11. Drag the toolbar back to its original location.

12. Right-click anywhere on or next to the **Common** toolbar to see a menu that shows the available toolbars.

You can click one of the toolbars in the menu to quickly make the toolbar available for an immediate task at hand, such as adding and managing content regions in a Microsoft .NET master page.

> **Note** The whole idea of all these different toolbars, and the ability to add or re-move buttons and customize them, is that Expression Web is designed to enable you to lay out your workspace the way that works best for you. Every designer works differently, and every project has slightly different work flow; so keep the flexibility of these toolbars and buttons in mind when you begin a new project. Spending 10 minutes customizing and arranging your toolbars can result in hours of time savings over the course of a sizable project. Trust me, the good folks at Microsoft didn't spend all the time required to make these toolbars so flexible just to show you what they can do. They did it so that you could save yourself time and have a workspace that meets your needs.

Toolbars, no matter how flexible or well thought out, are limited by their very nature. What happens if you have some kind of functionality that requires a level of complexity that simply can't be handled by a button? Enter the pane.

> **Tip** Twelve toolbars are available for display in the workspace, including the default Common toolbar and the menu bar. Each of the additional toolbars can help you work faster; but they do occupy screen space, so you probably won't want to have them open all the time.

13. On the menu bar, click **Task Panes**.

You will see a long list of available panes.

The groups of panes are separated by horizontal lines. Each group of panes between the horizontal lines will appear in the same pane area.

14. On the **Task Panes** menu, click **CSS Properties**.

You will see the CSS Properties task pane in the lower-left corner of your workspace.

15. Click **Task Panes** again.

You'll see a check mark by CSS Properties but no check mark by Tag Properties.

16. Click **Tag Properties**, and you'll reverse the situation.

Manipulating which panel is visible within a task pane isn't solely limited to the Task Panes menu. If you examine a task pane closely, you will see that there are tabs near the top of it.

These tabs represent the various panes that are available within that particular group.

17. On the **Task Panes** menu, click **Data Source Library**, **Data Source Details**, and **Conditional Formatting** to add these task panes to the **Toolbox** task group. Examine each of these panes, and then click **Toolbox** on the **Task Panes** menu to bring that pane to the top of the group.

18. Look at the **Toolbox** task pane group (located by default in the upper-right section of your workspace).

You'll see several tabs at the top of the pane. There is an arrow that enables you to scroll through the different tabs within the pane. You'll also see a button that enables you to maximize the pane and a button to close the pane.

19. Drag one of the tabs and release it over the center of your workspace so that it floats.

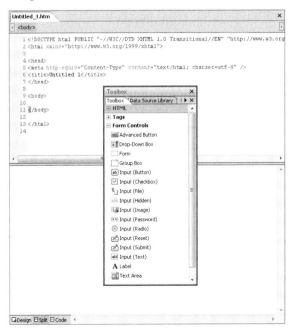

20. Drag the tab to any side of the workspace so that it is docked.

21. Repeat steps 19 and 20 using a few of the task panes. Give some thought to how you might like your workspace to be laid out.

22. On the **Task Panes** menu, click **Reset Workspace Layout** (at the bottom of the menu) to reset the panes to their original state.

23. On the **File** menu, click **Close** to close the *Untitled_1.htm* file that was created when you opened Expression Web in step 1 of this exercise.

You have now seen all of the options that are available to you in Expression Web. With all of the customizations and options in the toolbars alone, the choices can become overwhelming. When you add the pane groups and all the possible panes they can contain, the sheer volume of available tools can compound this issue. Keep in mind that all of these available tools are there to allow you to set up the workspace so that it suits your work flow or a specific task.

> **Tip** A third-party application that provides a greatly enhanced level of control over all of the panes in Expression Web is available from *www.panemanager.com*.

Opening an Existing Site

An *Expression Web site* will consist of a logical grouping of folders that contain all of the pages, images, and other files that make up the site. In most cases the site will also contain *metadata* that enables Expression Web to recognize when files were changed, to update references to files you might have renamed or replaced, the location to which the site has been published, and an array of other data the program can use for behind-the-scenes management.

In this exercise, you will learn to open and examine an entire site by using Expression Web.

> **Troubleshooting** On the File menu, there is a significant difference between clicking Open and clicking Open Site. Clicking Open Site will open an entire site within Expression Web, thereby enabling automatic hyperlink updates, publishing capabilities, and so on.
>
> Clicking Open will open only a single file. Any changes that are made to this file do not affect any other files. In most cases, clicking Open Site will be the preferred action.

 USE the *CH1* sample site. This sample site is located in the *Documents\Microsoft Press\Expression Web SBS\Sample Sites* folder.

1. On the **File** menu, click **Open Site**. In the **Open Site** dialog box, browse to *Documents\Microsoft Press\Expression Web SBS\Sample Sites*, and then click *CH1*.

2. Click **Open** to open the site in Expression Web.

   The site contains one of the personal Web site templates that come with Expression Web.

   With a full site open, you will see the Folder List on the left side of your workspace that has all the files and folders that make up your site. The main window will be set in Folders view.

   > **Tip** Folders view is very convenient for examining, managing, and modifying site structure. If you rename a folder, Expression Web will automatically update all of the internal links and references to it. When you're designing a site from scratch, it is a good idea to use Folders view for designing the overall architecture and folder structure for the site.

3. Click one of the subfolders in your **Folder List** on the left.

The Folders view to the right will show the contents of that folder.

4. Click the *root folder* in the **Folder List**.

All of the site's files and subfolders will reappear in your main workspace.

Displaying Different Views of a Site

In addition to the default Folders view, Expression Web provides a number of other views to assist in designing and managing a site.

In Expression Web, when a site is open but no individual files are open, four views will be available at the bottom of your main workspace: Folders, Remote Web Site, Reports, and Hyperlinks.

In this exercise, you will set up a remote Web site and examine it on a folder level.

USE the *CH1* sample site. This sample site is located in the *Documents\Microsoft Press\ Expression Web SBS\Sample Sites* folder.

OPEN the *CH1* sample site.

1. Click the **Web Site** tab at the top of the workspace to switch to **Web Site** view.

2. Right-click the white space in your main workspace.

You'll see options in the context menu for New and Arrange.

Tip These commands are the ones that are most often needed in this view. From the New submenu, you can select various types of new files or even a new folder. From the Arrange submenu, you can select many different ways to arrange the files that you see in Folders view. When you are working on a large site, using these different criteria to arrange the files in your workspace makes it easier for you to navigate and to find particular files quickly.

3. Click **Remote Web Site View** at the bottom of your main workspace.

You will see an empty view and a prompt to set up a *remote Web site*.

4. In the upper-right corner of the workspace, click **Remote Web Site Properties**.

The Remote Web Site Properties dialog box opens.

5. Select **File System** as your remote Web server type.

6. Open *Documents\Expression Web SBS\Sample Sites\Publish\CH1*, which will be your remote site.

7. Click **Reports** at the bottom of your main workspace.

Expression Web displays the default Site Summary report containing a variety of statistical information about your site.

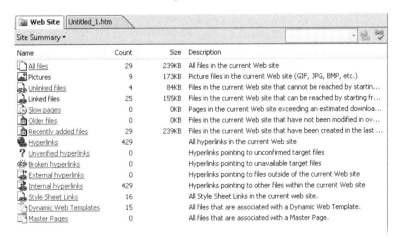

8. Click the **Site Summary** arrow above your main workspace.

All of the various reports are available from the menu that appears.

9. Click each available report on the menu and examine it.

10. Click **Hyperlinks** at the bottom of your main workspace.

11. Select a page from the **Folder List** to display the page and its linked files in the main workspace.

Files that show in Hyperlinks view with a plus sign (+) can be clicked to expand them and show all the files they link to.

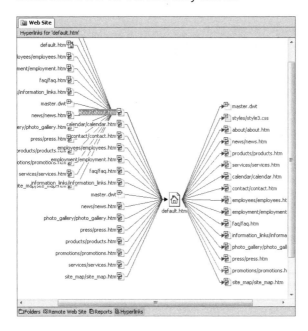

> **Tip** Hyperlinks view is very useful for figuring out where a file is used within a site, understanding how the site's overall navigation works, and other situations where you need either a big-picture overview of an entire site or a tight view of a particular file's purpose within a site.

Exploring an Individual Web Page

In the previous section, you opened a site and examined it on a folder level. In this exercise, you will open a page within this site, examine it at a page level, and use Expression Web's tools for editing files.

> **USE** the *CH1* sample site. This site is located in the *Documents\Microsoft Press\Expression Web SBS\Sample Sites* folder.
>
> **OPEN** the *CH1* sample site.

1. In the **Folder List**, double-click **default.htm**.

The home page of the sample site opens in the Expression Web workspace.

2. Point to the page header and page footer.

The pointer changes from an insertion point to a no-insertion-point icon, because the page is attached to a Dynamic Web Template.

> **Note** Dynamic Web Templates (DWT) are Expression Web's preferred method of keeping static pages within pages unified under a common look. In fact, every single site template that comes with Expression Web uses DWT to control the content pages. DWT works when you save files on your local computer, so there are no specific server requirements.

Save

3. There are two editable regions that you can work within on this page. Change the text in each of them, and then click the **Save** button.

At the bottom of the design surface, you will see three view buttons: Design, Split, and Code.

⟐Design ⊟Split ⊡Code

4. Click **Split**.

Split view shows both Code and Design views simultaneously.

5. Adjust the size of each view by dragging the separator between them up or down.

6. Select some text in the **Design** pane at the bottom of your workspace.

Notice how the Design view selection is also selected in the Code view pane.

7. In the **Folder List**, double-click the *master.dwt* file to open it. Change one of the phone numbers in the header.

Along the top of your Code pane, you'll see the quick tag selector bar. Notice the arrow on the tag when you pause the mouse pointer over it.

8. Click the arrow to see some options you can use.

9. Save the page.

You will be asked whether you want the pages that are attached to the DWT to be updated.

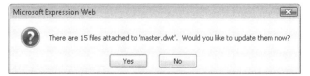

10. Click **Yes**, and then click **Close** on the confirmation box.

11. Set the mouse pointer in the navigation bar in the Design surface by clicking the link for Home.

If you look at the quick tag selector bar from right to left, you will see that the Home link is inside of an <a> tag that's inside an <li> and <ul> tag, which is inside a series of nested <div> tags.

> **Tip** The quick tag selector bar, Split view, and the CSS Properties task pane are indispensable tools for deeply exploring a complex document. With these tools, you can accurately and quickly find an exact place in a document's code structure, which is useful for designing, repairing, or modifying pages.

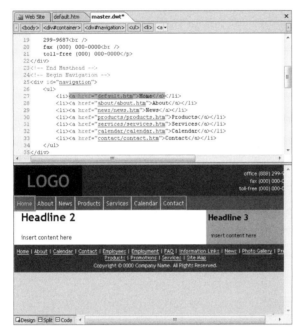

12. Point to each of the tags on the quick tag selector bar slowly from left to right.

Notice that when you point to a tag, a blue border appears around the corresponding element in the Design pane.

13. In the quick tag selector bar, click **div#navigation** to select that page element.

Notice that the containing element is a <div> tag.

> **Tip** All of Expression Web's supplied templates use completely *table-free* cascading style sheet layouts in addition to being based on a DWT template. Expression Web provides a number of tools to work with the cascading style sheets that control the layout and presentation of the page.

14. Click the **Home** link in the page's navigation bar.

Show set
properties
on top

15. On the **Task Panes** menu, click **CSS Properties**. On the **CSS Properties** task pane, make sure the **Show set properties on top** button is selected in order to show all of the CSS elements pertaining to that link stacked at the top of the CSS Properties task pane.

16. Expand the **margin** item in the **CSS Properties** task pane by clicking the plus sign (+) beside the item.

From here you can quickly change the whole cascading style sheet presentation of an element. All elements that are styled are highlighted in the CSS Properties task pane.

 CLOSE the *CH1* sample site and exit Expression Web.

You've now seen how Expression Web works with pages on an individual level, from both a code and design standpoint, and you've had a chance to work with Expression Web's tools. You've also seen how Expression Web's site templates rely on Dynamic Web Templates and cascading style sheets for layout and style.

Understanding Basic Expression Web Concepts

With Expression Web, you have virtually limitless possibilities for setting up your workspace, and you can chose to use or not use *proprietary technology* such as metafiles. Expression Web's overriding predisposition is to write W3C valid code and produce accessible sites, all while not forcing you to wade through HTML code.

You will also find Dynamic Web Templates to be an efficient way to manage Web sites and keep them uniform and uniformly updated.

Expression Web makes a distinction, and so should you, about what is an individual file and what is a file that's part of a logical grouping: an Expression Web site.

While Expression Web is an excellent tool for working on documents at any level from presentation to their code structure, if you understand and make use of the Expression Web "site" concept, you can use Expression Web's excellent site management capabilities.

Key Points

- Expression Web is the Web design component of *Microsoft Expression Studio* that replaces Microsoft Office FrontPage.

- The tools in Expression Web—toolbars, panes, and various Site views—can be easily customized to match your work flow.

- There is a distinct difference between a single file that exists or is opened from outside of an Expression Web site and a file that's opened from within an Expression Web site.

- Expression Web's tools let you easily find the exact place in a document's structural code by using synchronized design and code panes.

- There are multiple views for sites and pages, which provides greater workspace efficiency.

- Dynamic Web Templates aid in keeping Web sites uniform and in keeping common content areas on pages attached to them in perfect synchronization.

- Expression Web is not only a great design and editing tool, but also a great site management tool.

Chapter at a Glance

Publish a backup copy of a site, **page 27**

Use FrontPage code in an Expression Web site, **page 38**

2 Moving from FrontPage to Expression Web

In this chapter, you will learn to:

✔ Understand the differences between Expression Web and FrontPage.

✔ Publish a backup copy of a site.

✔ Manage FrontPage sites by using Expression Web.

✔ Use FrontPage code in an Expression Web site.

✔ Convert FrontPage sites to Expression Web.

Microsoft Office FrontPage was developed a decade ago, and 10 years is a long lifetime for a technology product. In its lifetime, FrontPage has gained many users, and this book would be remiss if it didn't give some serious and specific help to former FrontPage users. Even if you were never a FrontPage user, you'll most likely, at some time, need to convert, modify, or manage a FrontPage Web site.

> **Note** Keep in mind that although the Expression Web interface bears a strong resemblance to the FrontPage interface, Expression Web is *not* the next version of FrontPage. Expression Web is an *alternative replacement* product from the same software manufacturer.

In this chapter, you will learn about some of the differences between Expression Web and FrontPage. Next you will learn how to manage and protect sites that were created in FrontPage. Then you'll learn how to implement some FrontPage features in Expression Web and how to convert a site developed in FrontPage to Expression Web.

> **Important** Before you can use the practice files in this chapter, you need to install them from the book's companion CD to their default location. See "Using the Book's CD" on page xiii for more information.

> **Troubleshooting** Graphics and operating system–related instructions in this book reflect the Windows Vista user interface. If your computer is running Windows XP and you experience trouble following the instructions as written, please refer to the "Information for Readers Running Windows XP" section at the beginning of this book.

Understanding the Differences Between Expression Web and FrontPage

Expression Web is designed to enable you to continue to manage and make minor edits to FrontPage sites, but Expression Web is also designed so that you will no longer use outdated FrontPage features. Expression Web abandons old and proprietary FrontPage features, and provides tools for current techniques supported by the World Wide Web Consortium (W3C), with *cross-platform* capabilities.

If you used FrontPage as only an editing, managing, or publishing tool, you'll have an easier time moving forward than those who relied more heavily on FrontPage features such as FrontPage *themes*, *navigation components*, or other "*Web Bots*" provided by FrontPage.

One of the first things you'll notice is that many items that might be familiar to you as a FrontPage user do not appear in the Expression Web menus.

Here's a partial list of the items that do not appear:

- FrontPage themes
- Shared borders
- Web components, including:
    - Dynamic effects
    - Hit counter
    - Photo gallery
    - Link bars
    - Included content
    - Other items that were found in the Web Component dialog box
- Navigation and Task views
- Database Results Wizard

You'll undoubtedly find that other items do not appear in their familiar menu locations.

The rationale behind the disappearance of many of these menu items is simple: They inserted non-W3C compliant code, required FrontPage Server Extensions, or both. Professional Web developers will not miss most of the absent menu items, and the replacement techniques and tools that Expression Web provides produce a much better Web site.

Publishing a Backup Copy of a Site

When you need to work on a FrontPage site, you should first protect it by creating a backup copy of the site. The best way to make the backup copy is by using the publishing feature.

> **Note** If you were previously a FrontPage user, it's a good idea to retain an installation of FrontPage. Situations might arise, for example, in which a customer doesn't want to move away from FrontPage navigation components or a theme and needs you to do some work on their existing FrontPage site.
>
> If you don't have FrontPage installed, you can't easily do various FrontPage proprietary tasks such as modifying FrontPage themes, manipulating pages in *Navigation view*, or working with the *Database Results Wizard*. Though Expression Web provides appropriate ways to perform all of these tasks, not all site owners will want to invest the time that would be required to carry out the improvements, or perhaps they like the simplicity of working with some of these proprietary FrontPage features.
>
> Even if you install Expression Web as an upgrade option for FrontPage, FrontPage will not be removed from your computer.

In this exercise, you will use Expression Web to back up a FrontPage site.

USE the *FrontPageExample* site. This practice site is located in the *Documents\Microsoft Press\Expression Web SBS\Sample Sites* folder.

BE SURE TO start Expression Web before beginning this exercise.

OPEN the *FrontPageExample* site by clicking Open Site on the File menu.

1. In Windows Explorer, create a folder location for publishing your backup, such as *Documents\My Web Sites\FPbackup*.

2. Switch to Expression Web. On the **File** menu, click **Publish Site**.

The Remote Web Site Properties dialog box opens.

3. On the **Remote Web Site** tab, click **File System**, and then click **Browse**. Browse to the folder you created in step 1, and then click **Open**. When Expression Web prompts you to confirm that you want to create a Web site at that location, click **Yes**.

You are now in *Remote Web Site* view in Expression Web.

4. In the lower-right corner of the workspace, click **Publish Web site**.

> **Troubleshooting** If you attempt to publish a site that has FrontPage features that rely on server-side code execution or *FrontPage Server extensions* to a disk-based location, you will get a warning alert. Because you're publishing to a disk-based location as a form of backup and not to allow browsing or functionality, click Ignore And Continue.

Expression Web publishes the site, creating a backup copy of the original FrontPage site on your computer.

  5. At the bottom of the work area, click the **Folders** button to view the files in the *FrontPageExample* site.

You can now do whatever you want with the open site in full confidence that it is a copy of the original site, and no harm can come to the original FrontPage site.

> **Important** The preceding process is the preferred method of moving, copying, or backing up any FrontPage Web site. You should use the publish method whether you are publishing from your server to your local computer or another server, or from a local file location to the server or to another file location. There are *metafiles* and hidden folder structures that must stay intact for continued reliability, and the publish method guarantees the best result.

Managing FrontPage Sites by Using Expression Web

Expression Web is a great tool for managing any kind of site, including those that were created in FrontPage.

Virtually any FrontPage feature can still be used through Expression Web. Most of the absent FrontPage features were simply removed from the user interface but are present beneath the surface. The logic here is that the Expression Web development team wanted former FrontPage users to be able to open pages, change text and images, and make other page-level modifications, but not necessarily to continue using the original features.

Even though Expression Web is nondestructive to Web sites that were created in FrontPage, it's still a good idea to back up FrontPage sites before modifying them.

If you need to make significant modifications to FrontPage components or themes, the best method will be to use FrontPage.

However, when you manage and publish FrontPage sites with Expression Web, you'll get the benefits of better syntax highlighting (based on the **DOCTYPE**), much better style sheet capabilities, and many other standards-based improvements.

The following exercises will acquaint you with using Expression Web to maintain and manage an existing FrontPage site.

Changing Shared Border Content

Here's the scenario: You need to change the content in a **shared border** in a FrontPage-created Web site. You don't want to do a full conversion to the site; you simply want to change some common content and then publish it.

In this exercise, you will replace FrontPage content in a shared border.

USE the *FrontPageExample* site you modified in the previous exercise. This practice site is located in the *Documents\Microsoft Press\Expression Web SBS\Sample Sites* folder.

OPEN the *FrontPageExample* site.

1. Open the *index.htm* page in Split view, and display the shared border at the bottom of the page.

For this example, you will change the e-mail address at the bottom of the page from *someone@microsoft.com* to *Mail@Example.com*.

> **Tip** Not only is the content you want to change inside a shared border, but it is also a *FrontPage substitution*. You simply want to replace it with a normal e-mail address and mailto hyperlink.

2. Click the **someone@microsoft.com** hyperlink to select it, and then press the ⟦Del⟧ key to remove both the hyperlink and the FrontPage substitution.

3. Type **Mail@Example.com** to replace the original hyperlink. Select the text you typed, right-click the selection, and then click **Hyperlink**.

   The Edit Hyperlink dialog box opens.

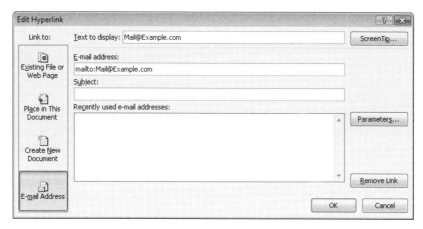

4. In the **Edit Hyperlink** dialog box, click **E-mail Address**, type the e-mail address and a message subject, and then click **OK**.

5. On the toolbar, click **Save**.

   Expression Web saves the changes to the page.

6. On the toolbar, click the **Preview in Browser** button to preview how visitors will see your change.

Save

Preview in
Browser

7. Click a few links and check the footer area of those pages to be sure that your change to the shared border updated the pages that receive that content

You've just successfully changed a FrontPage proprietary feature from within the design surface of Expression Web. In the next exercise, you'll make a change to an even more FrontPage-centric element from a less than apparent facility in Expression Web.

Adding a Page

Here's the scenario: You need to create a new page and add it to your existing Navigation view and link bars that were originally created in FrontPage. The best method would be to open the relevant site in FrontPage, create the new page, and add it to the Navigation view. However, this exercise assumes that FrontPage isn't available to you.

> **Important** Navigation view does not appear in the Expression Web interface. It has been removed to discourage continued use because the link bars it generates are not valid HTML. In the following exercise, you'll temporarily bring back the Navigation view to add a page so that it will be included in the site's existing link bars. It is strongly recommended that you use this method very sparingly and only in situations where it is absolutely necessary.

In this exercise, you will create a page and add it to your existing Navigation view and link bars.

USE the *FrontPageExample* site you modified in the previous exercise. This practice site is located in the *Documents\Microsoft Press\Expression Web SBS\Sample Sites* folder.

OPEN the *FrontPageExample* site.

1. In the **Folder List**, right-click **prod03.htm**, click **Copy**, right-click the root folder, and then click **Paste**.

   Expression Web creates a file named *prod03_copy(1).htm* in the root folder.

2. Right-click the **prod03_copy(1).htm** file, click **Rename**, type **prod04.htm**, and then press [Enter].

   The Folder List displays the *prod04.htm* file in the list.

3. In the **Folder List**, double-click **prod04.htm** to open it in Design view. Right-click the Design surface of the page, whether in Design or Split view, and then click **Page Properties**.

4. In the **Page Properties** dialog box, change the page title to **Adventure Works Product 4**.

5. Click **OK** to close the **Page Properties** dialog box.

6. On the toolbar, click **Save**.

> **Note** You have now created, renamed, and changed the page title of a *very* FrontPage proprietary site. You'll notice that many of the page elements are showing notices about adding them to Navigation view to display the *link bars* and page banners.

In order to use your newly created page, you'll need to get Navigation view back temporarily.

7. On the **Tools** menu, click **Macro**, and then click *Visual Basic Editor.*

The Microsoft Visual Basic Editor starts.

8. In the Visual Basic Editor, click **View**, and then click **Immediate Window**. In the **Immediate** window pane, type the following code:

```
ActiveWebWindow.ViewMode = WebViewNavigation
```

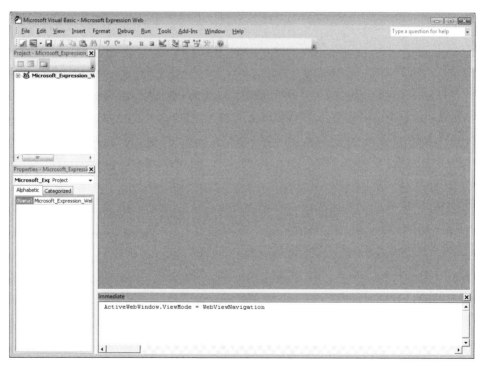

9. Press ⌈Enter⌋ to run the code.

In Expression Web, you'll see a representation of Navigation view.

10. Drag the **prod04.htm** page you created in step 2 into the **Navigation** pane, and drop it immediately to the right of Product 3. Right-click the page icon, click **Rename**, and then type **Product 4**.

11. In the **Navigation** pane, double-click the **Product 4** page icon to open the page for editing.

You'll notice that the page has the same elements as its sibling pages.

12. On the toolbar, click **Preview** to view this page as a visitor would see it. In the browser, navigate to a few of the other product pages to verify that your changes in the preceding steps have created a uniform page.

 CLOSE the *FrontPageExample* site and the Visual Basic Editor.

By using the preceding method, you can make minor changes to sites that rely heavily on FrontPage's navigation structure for elements such as navigation bars, *page banners*, and other elements that require the now obsolete FrontPage Navigation view.

It's important to use the method for only quick changes to a site that isn't ready for a full conversion to Expression Web. It would be counterproductive to use discontinued features such as Navigation view on new sites, especially because Expression Web has so many tools to make use of superior techniques.

Using FrontPage Code in an Expression Web Site

Though the majority of FrontPage proprietary features are absent from Expression Web because they don't create valid code, there might be a few occasions when you will want to use one or two of these features. For example, one that doesn't have any negative aspects such as not being cross-browser compatible or requiring anything special on the server is the FrontPage Included Content Web component. This Web component simply copied all of the content between the <body> and </body> tags of one page in a Web site and wrote it into another page or set of pages. It was similar to a server-side include but worked at *save time* instead.

This feature was good for actions such as inserting a menu into a number of pages. By using a FrontPage Include, you'd need to maintain or modify the code in only one page and its changes would be reflected in all pages that used its content.

In this exercise, you will add the code for a FrontPage Include to your *Code Snippets list* in Expression Web.

> **USE** the *CH2* site. This practice site is located in the *Documents\Microsoft Press\Expression Web SBS\Sample Sites* folder.
> **OPEN** the *CH2* site.

1. Open the *default.htm* page. If you're not in Split view, click the **Split View** button at the bottom of the workspace.

2. In the Design pane, click to place the *insertion point* just after the *2* in **Heading 2**, and then press ⌷Enter⌷ to create a new paragraph.

3. From the site's *Extras* folder, open the file *CodeSnippets.txt*, and copy the following line of code to the clipboard:

   ```
   <!--webbot bot="Include" U-Include="Double Click and Browse to a Page"
   TAG="BODY" -->
   ```

4. In the Code pane, with the insertion point in the new paragraph you created in step 2, press ⌷Ctrl⌷+⌷Enter⌷ to open the Code Snippets list, and then double-click **Customize list**.

   The Page Editor Options dialog box opens with the Code Snippets tab active.

5. Click **Add**. In the **Add Code Snippet** dialog box that opens, enter **FPinclude** in the **Keyword** box, enter **Savetime Include** in the **Description** box, and paste the copied code snippet into the **Text** box.

6. Click **OK** in the **Add Code Snippet** dialog box and then in the **Page Editor Options** dialog box, to save your changes and return to the workspace.

7. Press Ctrl + Enter to open the Code Snippets list, and then type **FPi**.

The corresponding snippet is selected.

8. Press Enter to insert the selected snippet on the page.

You now have an Include Page in Design view.

9. In the Design pane, double-click the text that represents the Included Content Web component to open the **Include Page Properties** dialog box. Click **Browse**, and then browse to the file *dummytext.htm* inside the site's *Extras* folder. Select the file, and click **OK**.

Expression Web writes the content from *dummytext.htm* into the home page of the site.

Now we will try the same technique with the *HTML Markup component*.

> **Tip** The HTML Markup component is useful to protect code from being modified in any way by FrontPage or Expression Web. Though it's labeled *HTML* markup, you can insert any code you want, such as *JavaScript*, *ASP*, *PHP*, and so on.
>
> To use the HTML Markup component, double-click it in the Design pane to open the HTML Markup dialog box, and paste or type the code you want to be protected into the text area.

10. Set the insertion point in the Design pane immediately after the include page you inserted, and press ⌷Enter⌷ to create a new paragraph.

11. Return to *CodeSnippets.txt*, and copy the following line of code to the clipboard:

```
<!--webbot bot="HTMLMarkup" startspan --><!--webbot bot="HTMLMarkup"
endspan -->
```

12. Repeat steps 4 through 6 to add the code to the Code Snippets list with a keyword of **FPmarkup** and a description of **Prevents code from being changed by Expression Web**. Then insert the code from the Code Snippets list into the blank paragraph you created in step 10.

> **Troubleshooting** In the event that you don't see a Web Component tag in the Design pane where you added this code snippet, on the View menu, click Formatting Marks, and then click Show.

 CLOSE the *CH2* site.

> **Tip**   If you can't find the exact place in your Source view where you want something to appear, just set the insertion point in the Design pane and type something easy to find such as ### or ~#~. When you display Source view, search for and highlight the characters you entered, and then paste, or insert from your Code Snippets list the code you want to enter.

The preceding procedures showed you two examples of FrontPage features that are worth keeping. Neither of them in and of itself requires anything special on the server and doesn't do anything invalid from a W3C validity point of view.

Converting FrontPage Sites to Expression Web

The first thing you need to consider when converting a FrontPage site to Expression Web is strategy. You need to plan what you will do to replace FrontPage link bars, shared borders, and themes. After these decisions are made, it will be fairly easy work.

See Also   For more information about converting a FrontPage site, see the *Microsoft_FrontPage_to_Expression_Web* document on the CD.

Interactive buttons in Expression Web are a good replacement for FrontPage link bars. Dynamic Web Templates can be used instead of *FrontPage shared borders*, and cascading style sheets are the obvious choice for replacing FrontPage themes. All of these Expression Web features are easy to use, and you'll reap benefits of HTML validity and accessibility, in addition to cross-browser and cross-platform usability.

There are a number of ways to convert a FrontPage site to a standards-based Expression Web site.

In this exercise, you will learn the conversion method that's most efficient from a workflow point of view, and you will dispose of all the old FrontPage content with a single click.

> **Important**   If you try to open a FrontPage site that contains themes and shared borders, every new page you create will inherit those elements. Trying to convert a FrontPage site this way is at worst a recipe for frustration and at best just not a very efficient way to work. The most efficient way to do a conversion is to create a new site with Expression Web and copy into it only the text and images from the FrontPage site.

USE the *FrontPageExample* site you modified earlier in this chapter. This practice site is located in the *Documents\Microsoft Press\Expression Web SBS\Sample Sites* folder.

OPEN the *FrontPageExample* site.

1. On the **File** menu, click **New**. In the **New** dialog box, click the **Web Site** tab. Click **Templates** in the left pane, and then click **Small Business 1** in the center pane.

2. Browse to the location where you want to locate the site, and then click **OK** to create it.

3. Arrange the pages and navigation of the site as you want, modify the style attributes if necessary, and generally build a new Web site for the old FrontPage site's content.

When you have the Web site template in Expression Web configured to your liking, you're just about ready to start migrating text, images, and other assets from the original FrontPage site.

> **Tip** To make things easier, you should have a copy of the old FrontPage site within the structure of the new site you created in step 1.

4. Open Windows Explorer and locate the *FrontPageExample* site that will provide
the content. Drag the folder containing the site into the root folder of your newly
created Web site.

5. In the message box warning you that directories containing Web site configuration
will not be imported, click **OK**.

The FrontPage site's files will be moved into your Expression Web site, and you can
easily copy content and provide easy access to the other assets you might still need.

As a result of the action you completed in step 4, all of the files and content
from your previous FrontPage site are available to you within your new
Expression Web site.

6. As you use images from the old site's folder structure, simply drag them into the
images folder of your Expression Web site. Do the same for any other asset you
want to reuse from the old site.

7. After you migrate all of your content into the new pages, delete the old FrontPage
folder structure, and you're ready to publish your Expression Web site.

CLOSE the open Web site. If you are not continuing directly to the next chapter, exit
Expression Web.

Important Assuming that your previous FrontPage site was published to a server,
it's highly recommended that you delete the files in that Web site before publishing the
Expression Web site to the same location. This removal can be accomplished by opening
the live site with Expression Web and deleting all of the files and folders from your old
FrontPage site or by contacting your hosting provider and having them remove all of
the files and folders from your hosting space.

Key Points

- Many FrontPage features are absent, but everything that's gone can be replaced in a better, more efficient, and standards-based way.

- Some FrontPage features that are absent from Expression Web can be brought back with little effort.

- You can convert an old, inefficient FrontPage site to take advantage of the new standards-based, cross-browser, and cross-platform type of site that Expression Web was designed to build.

- You can protect an original FrontPage site by publishing it to a *local folder*.

- Though not all FrontPage features can be added to new sites created in Expression Web, all existing FrontPage sites can be managed and published with Expression Web.

- Elements that require proprietary FrontPage features should not be used; they should be fondly remembered relics.

Chapter at a Glance

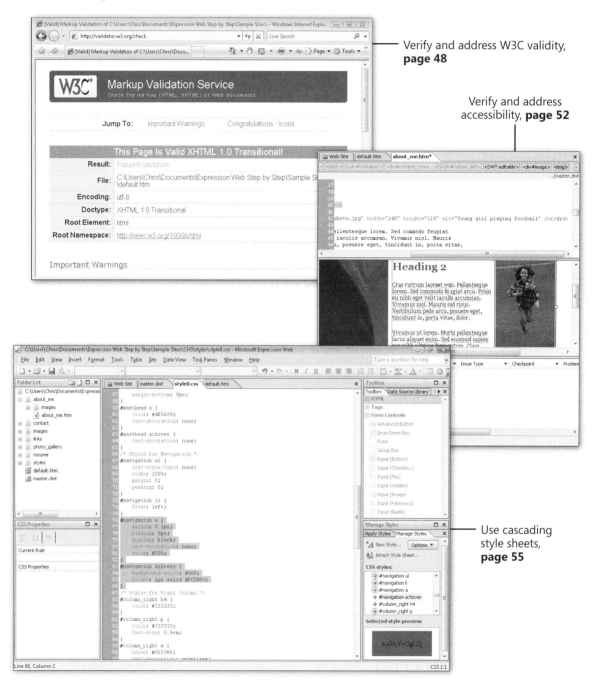

Verify and address W3C validity,
page 48

Verify and address
accessibility, **page 52**

Use cascading
style sheets,
page 55

3 Becoming Familiar with Modern Web Site Standards

In this chapter, you will learn to:

- ✔ Verify and address W3C validity.
- ✔ Verify and address accessibility.
- ✔ Use cascading style sheets.
- ✔ Choose and use the right DOCTYPE.
- ✔ Verify and improve cross-browser rendering.

Today's modern Internet emphasizes several key principals: validity, accessibility, cross-browser compatibility, and a clean separation of content and presentation. You will be glad to know that Expression Web provides you with the tools you'll need to accomplish Web site development based on modern Web standards and best practices, and actually makes development easy.

For most of the key principals, you don't need to be an expert in behind-the-scenes code, because Expression Web will either automatically ensure these principals are followed, or provide you with a visual interface.

In this chapter, you will learn to verify World Wide Web Consortium (W3C) validity and to check and address accessibility. You will also learn to use cascading style sheets and to choose and use the right Document Type Declaration (DOCTYPE). Finally, you will learn to check and improve cross-browser rendering.

Important Before you can use the practice files in this chapter, you need to install them from the book's companion CD to their default location. See "Using the Book's CD" on page xiii for more information.

Troubleshooting Graphics and operating system–related instructions in this book reflect the Windows Vista user interface. If your computer is running Windows XP and you experience trouble following the instructions as written, please refer to the "Information for Readers Running Windows XP" section at the beginning of this book.

Verifying and Addressing W3C Validity

You can visit the W3C Web site at *w3c.org*. One of the functions of W3C is to maintain a base of standards that define valid code. Expression Web is predisposed to meet those standards by writing valid HTML/XHTML code.

In this exercise, you will verify the validity of code, and you will set up a problem and fix it.

BE SURE TO start Expression Web.

USE the *CH3* site. This practice site is located in the *Documents\Microsoft Press\Expression Web SBS\Sample Sites* folder.

OPEN the *CH3* site and display the *default.htm* page.

Preview

1. On the toolbar, click **Preview** to open the page in Windows Internet Explorer (provided that is your default Web browser). Open another tab in your browser or open another browser window and go to *validator.w3.org*. Click the **Validate by File Upload** tab, click **Browse,** navigate to and double-click the local copy of this page, and then click **Check**.

A copy of your local page is forwarded to the W3C's validation engine, which reports that the page is fully valid.

> **Tip** To save time, instead of browsing to the page on your local system, you can copy the URL from the address bar in the browser preview you opened and paste it into the file field.

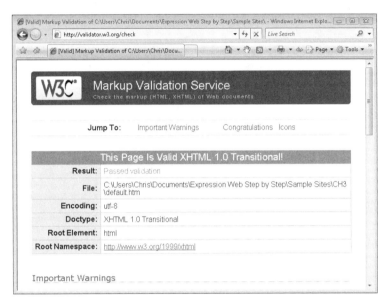

2. Close the browser or browsers, and return to Expression Web. Click **Split** at the bottom of the workspace to display the page in Split view.

   Because Expression Web won't let you make validity mistakes through Design view, you'll need to make a mistake manually in the code.

3. Set the insertion point in front of the first **<p>** tag in the main editable region, and add an erroneous extra <p>. Expression Web, in an effort to maintain validity, will automatically close the <p> tag (or any open tag, for that matter). Delete the </p> tag it inserts to create the error.

Validity rules dictate that you can't have nested <p> tags and must close the open tag before adding another.

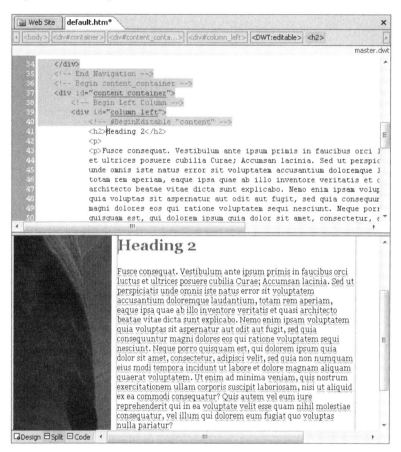

4. Save the page, and then preview it once more. Again, open another tab in your browser or open another browser window and go to *validator.w3.org*. Click the **Validate by File Upload** tab, click **Browse**, double-click the local copy of this page, and then click **Check**.

Notice that the page now fails because of the extra <p> tag.

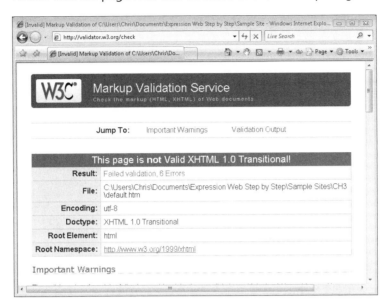

5. Close the browser window or windows and return to Expression Web.

Notice that the second <p> tag has a red line beneath it. When you have code in Expression Web that violates the standards of the document's DOCTYPE declaration, you'll see this red line under the invalid tags. If you pause the mouse pointer over one of these underlined tags, Expression Web shows you a tip that explains what's wrong with the underlined tag.

6. To see this validation process in effective use, open the FrontPage example site from this book's CD, and run it through the W3C validation engine by using the method you just tried above.

You'll be shocked by how badly the site fails validation.

 CLOSE the open browser windows.

Verifying and Addressing Accessibility

Accessibility relates to the way a page is structured and how it will render in devices that are used by people who have vision problems or who need other special browser considerations.

Good HTML/XHTML practices such as using valid code and meaningful *alt tags*, and not relying on JavaScript or Flash for key elements such as navigation will prevent most accessibility problems.

In this exercise, you will create code that violates accessibility standards, and then you will repair the error.

> **USE** the *CH3* site. This practice site is located in the *Documents\Microsoft Press\Expression Web SBS\Sample Sites* folder.
>
> **OPEN** the *CH3* site and display the *default.htm* page.

1. On the **Tools** menu, click **Accessibility Reports** to open the Accessibility Checker.

2. Using the default Accessibility Checker settings, click **Check**.

   The Accessibility task pane opens below the Design pane and shows errors that exist in the open page.

3. Close the **Accessibility** task pane.

   Because you're not going to find any errors in this Expression Web template, you will need to create an error.

4. In the **Folder List**, expand the **about_me** folder, and then open the **about_me.htm** page. If your screen is not in Split view, click the **Split View** button at the bottom of the workspace.

5. Select the image that is in the Design pane, and find the code for the image in the Code pane. In the tag for that image, remove the alt attribute (*alt=""*).

Accessibility rules dictate that every image must have an *alt* attribute even if the attribute is empty, as shown in this page.

6. On the toolbar, click **Save**. On the **Tools** menu, click **Accessibility Reports** to open the Accessibility Checker, and then click **Check**.

An error is now visible in the Accessibility task pane.

Rather than simply replacing the previously removed, empty *alt* attribute, let's put something meaningful there.

7. Set the insertion point immediately in front of the closing image tag that you modified in step 5, type **alt="Young girl playing football"**, and click **Save**.

Refresh

8. In the **Accessibility** task pane, click **Refresh**.

The error no longer appears.

> **Note** You can generate a report by clicking Generate HTML Report in the Accessibility task pane. Expression Web generates a new page that has the errors reported. This report can be generated for a page, for a selection of pages, or for a site, and is a valuable tool when redesigning or analyzing a site. You can save or print the report for your own records or for your customer.

Using Cascading Style Sheets

A cornerstone of modern Web standards and practices is the separation of content from presentation. Expression Web helps you with this separation by leaning strongly toward cascading style sheets for presentational tasks such as formatting text and creating visual elements for your layout.

In this exercise, you will modify some of the cascading style sheet elements in the Dynamic Web Template.

USE the *CH3* site. This practice site is located in the *Documents\Microsoft Press\Expression Web SBS\Sample Sites* folder.

OPEN the *CH3* site and the *master.dwt* file.

1. Select the navigation bar at the top of the page. If necessary, set your insertion point in the navigation bar, and then click the **<div #navigation>** entry on the quick tag selector.

   The entire <div #navigation> element is selected.

   ```
   Web Site    master.dwt                                                    ×
   <body>  <div#container>  <div#navigation>  <ul>  <li>  <a>
   19            <h1><a href="#">Website Name</a></h1>
   20            <h3>Website description</h3>
   21        </div>
   22        <!-- End Masthead -->
   23        <!-- Begin Navigation -->
   24        <div id="navigation">
   25            <ul>
   26                <li><a href="default.htm">Home</a></li>
   27                <li><a href="about_me/about_me.htm">About Me</a></li>
   28                <li><a href="resume/resume.htm">Résumé</a></li>
   29                <li><a href="photo_gallery/photo_gallery.htm">Photo Gallery</a></li
   30                <li><a href="links/links.htm">Links</a></li>
   31                <li><a href="contact/contact.htm">Contact</a></li>
   32            </ul>
   33        </div>
   34        <!-- End Navigation -->
   ```

2. In the **CSS Properties** task pane on the left, under **Applied Rules**, click **#navigation** for style0.css, and then in the **CSS Properties** task pane, note the grey style (#DCDBE0) next to **background-color**.

   > **Important** When working in the CSS Properties task pane, it's important to select Show Set Properties On Top. By doing this, you'll stack all of the properties that have been specifically styled at the top of the list and you won't have to search through the entire list to find the style you're looking for.

3. Click **background-color**, and then click the **background-color** arrow to show the **Color Selector**. Click **More Colors**, and then click **Select**.

4. Pause the eye dropper over the image to the left of the navigation bar in the page's design surface, and pick up the color of the image area that is adjacent to the navigation bar.

5. Click **OK** to accept your selection.

The background color of the navigation bar changes. There are more style rules in play for that navigation bar than the color of the DIV element that contains it.

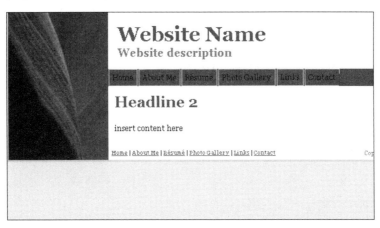

6. When the navigation DIV element is selected, point to the other elements on the quick tag selector bar to see how they relate to the irregular area within that DIV element: <ul>, <li>, and <a>.

Notice that when the pointer is over the A element, the culprit is visible.

7. On the quick tag selector bar, click **<a>** to display its properties in the **CSS Properties** task pane.

8. Delete the text to the right of the top entry for the **border** style to remove the borders and border colors for the **#navigation a** style.

The navigation bar is now starting to look more uniform.

9. On the toolbar, click **Save**. Allow Expression Web to update all of the pages that the Dynamic Web Template is attached to, and allow the style sheet to be saved.

10. Display the *default.htm* page, and view the presentation of this Dynamic Web Template's elements, then preview the page in your browser. Notice that the navigation bar looks uniform. Now point to the links in the navigation bar. They don't look very uniform.

11. In Expression Web, open the *master.dwt* file. To remedy the consistency issues in the navigation bar, and for a better workflow, double-click the **#navigation a** entry in the **Manage Styles** task pane.

Your style sheet opens, with the selected style ID in focus.

12. On the style sheet, look for the entry **#navigation a: hover.** This entry controls the link's appearance when you point to it. Remove the following line of code:

```
border: 1px solid #DCDBE0;
```

13. Save your style sheet, and then switch to *default.htm* to preview the file in your browser.

Notice that the navigation bar is starting to take shape and is looking more uniform. The borders are gone from the A element both when you point to it and when you don't.

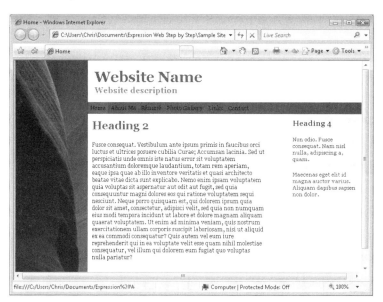

14. In Expression Web, switch to *master.dwt*. On the quick tag selector, in the navigation <div> element, click **<a>**. In the **CSS Properties** task pane, scroll down to **Color**.

Notice that the setting is a dark color.

15. Select the color entry to open the **Color selector**, and change the **color** attribute to a lighter color.

16. Save the Dynamic Web Template, and when prompted, save the style sheet. Switch to *default.htm*, and then click **Preview** to view the file in Internet Explorer. Point to the navigation links.

The navigation links now have a uniform appearance. They all have the lighter text color and lack the border.

17. Close your browser. In Expression Web, switch to *master.dwt*. In the Design pane, set the insertion point in the editable region on the right, and click the **<div #column_right>** tag on the quick tag selector.

18. In the **CSS Properties** task pane, scroll to **background**, and change the color value from **#F7F7F9** to **#D7DCDF**, which is more appropriate for this page.

19. Click **Save** to save your changes to the Dynamic Web Template. Allow Expression Web to update all of the pages that the Dynamic Web Template is attached to, and allow the style sheet to be saved.

20. Switch to *default.htm*, preview the page in a browser, and review your changes. Notice that there is now a silver background for the right-hand column. Click the navigation links to review all of the pages.

CLOSE the open browser windows.

During the preceding exercise, you made global changes to the presentation of every page in a site by simply editing a few lines on a style sheet. You edited the style sheet's code both directly and by using Expression Web's user interface. Though it might seem trivial on such a small site, think about how effective this method would be on sites with thousands of pages!

Imagine changing the link colors or other elements in every single page by simply editing one line in one single file. In addition, imagine how much less code is required for this type of arrangement than endless *<font>* tags to control presentation within the page code itself.

This is the just tip of the iceberg in regard to separation of content and presentation.

Choosing and Using the Right DOCTYPE

A DOCTYPE is a declaration at the very beginning of an HTML/XHTML file that tells the browser what kind of document it's receiving. A valid DOCTYPE is the very first thing you need to make sure your page(s) will validate.

In addition to making a page valid, there's an added benefit to a correct DOCTYPE: predictable browser rendering. To deliver consistent display in all browsers, the browser needs to be told what kind of file it's displaying.

> **Troubleshooting**   By default, Expression Web inserts an XHTML 1.0 Transitional DOCTYPE on every page it creates and ensures that the code is appropriate for the DOCTYPE. The only time you need to consider the DOCTYPE is when you're working on an existing site that was created by using another program or in a situation where you want to use a different DOCTYPE than the standard one that Expression Web provides.

In this exercise, you will change the DOCTYPE of a file and then validate it.

> **USE** the *CH3* site. This practice site is located in the *Documents\Microsoft Press\Expression Web SBS\Sample Sites* folder.
>
> **OPEN** the *CH3* site, and display the *default.htm* page in Split view.

1. At the top of the code pane, locate the following DOCTYPE information:

   ```
   <!DOCTYPE html PUBLIC "-//W3C//DTD XHTML 1.0 Transitional//EN" "http://www.
   w3.org/TR/xhtml1/DTD/xhtml1-transitional.dtd">
   ```

2. In the Code pane, select the DOCTYPE, and then press Ctrl + Enter to open the Code Snippets list.

Notice the seven different DOCTYPEs that are available from the Code Snippets list.

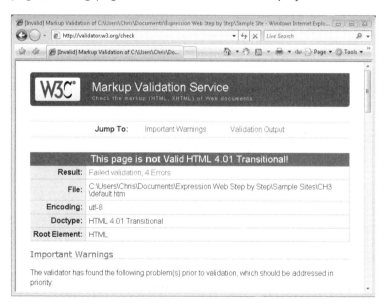

3. Select the **HTML 4.01 Transitional DOCTYPE**, click **Save**, and then preview the page in a browser.

The preview page appears to be the same as when you first opened it.

4. Open another tab in your browser or open another browser window and go to *validator.w3.org*. Click the **Validate by File Upload** tab, click **Browse**, double-click the local copy of this page, and then click **Check**. Instead of the previously valid page, a failing page with four errors is now displayed.

5. Close the browser, and in Expression Web, display the *default.htm* page.

Examine the Code pane, and notice the red underline beneath items that don't match the DOCTYPE you selected in step 3.

6. In the Code pane, select the DOCTYPE, press [Ctrl]+[Enter] to open the Code Snippets list, and click **XHTML 1.0 Transitional DOCTYPE** to return the page to its original state.

 CLOSE any open browser windows.

> **Troubleshooting** The DOCTYPE of a file in Expression Web dictates the IntelliSense, compatibility, validity, and accessibility testing rules. If you change a DOCTYPE, Expression Web changes the way it treats the page code. Don't conclude, however, that using a looser or lower DOCTYPE is a cure for old sites that you're trying to clean up by using Expression Web. Generally, it's best to add a modern DOCTYPE and bring the code up to that standard.

Verifying and Improving Cross-Browser Rendering

Cross-browser rendering simply means how a page renders in different browsers. Generally, you want a Web page to render identically in all modern browsers. Sometimes getting an absolutely identical rendering requires more work than it's worth, so what you should really concentrate on is getting an acceptable rendering across all common browsers.

Methods that you might use to obtain an absolutely identical rendering might cause problems when any of the browsers that are involved are updated or change versions, and you would need to repair whatever you did to obtain the identical rendering.

The solution is to make sure that your pages are valid and accessible, and that they render well across major browsers. This approach will stand the test of time.

> **Troubleshooting** In order to test your pages in browsers other than Internet Explorer, you must have the other browsers installed on your computer. For most testing, you can use Internet Explorer and Mozilla Firefox. Occasionally, you will want to also test in the Opera browser. Generally, if a page looks good in Internet Explorer and Firefox, it will look acceptable with most other browsers.
>
> Download at least one of the following browsers:
>
> ● Firefox: *www.mozilla.com/firefox/*
> ● Opera: *www.opera.com/download/*
>
> When you install a new browser, be sure to choose custom installation where offered. Ensure that the new browser does not become your default browser, and that you don't make any system changes unless that's what you truly want!

In this exercise, you will view a Web site in multiple browsers and address cross-browser inconsistencies.

USE the *CH3* site. This practice site is located in the *Documents\Microsoft Press\Expression Web SBS\Sample Sites* folder.

BE SURE TO download and install the alternative browsers as described in the preceding Troubleshooting paragraph before starting this exercise.

OPEN the *CH3* site and display the *default.htm* page.

1. On the **File** menu, click **Preview in Browser**, and then click **Edit Browser List**. Make sure that your newly loaded browsers are displayed in the list, and select their check boxes to make them available on the **Preview** list.

Troubleshooting If an installed browser is not displayed in the browser list, click Add. In the Add Browser dialog box, click Browse, browse to the Program Files folder to locate the browser you're looking for, and select it. Repeat the process for additional browsers as needed. When the browser list is as you want it, close all running instances of Expression Web, and then restart Expression Web.

2. On the **File** menu, click **Preview in Multiple Browsers**.

The *default.htm* page opens in all of the browsers you added in step 1. Compare the preview of the page in each of the browsers that opened. Make sure to point to links and navigate through the pages in each browser.

If you see an unacceptable inconsistency, you need to find that area in your page by using Design view and Split view, and use deductive reasoning to solve the problem. For example, if the problem is a deficient or excess application of padding on a certain element, then you'll probably need to find that element's style in the style sheet and remove or increase padding.

3. In Expression Web, with *default.htm* open for editing, on the **Tools** menu, click **Compatibility Reports**.

The Compatibility Checker dialog box opens.

4. Select the option for **All pages**, **Open page(s)**, **Selected pages**, or **Current page**. Select which browser you want the HTML/XHTML compatibility checked with, and which version of cascading style sheets you want the compatibility checked with, and then click **Check**.

The Compatibility Checker checks the code of the page and displays a report in the lower portion of your workspace. The checker defaults to checking against Microsoft Internet Explorer 6. Using the Compatibility Checker is a good way to check for flaws that cause rendering problems in any browser.

CLOSE the *CH3* site and the open browser windows. If you are not continuing directly to the next chapter, exit Expression Web.

Note You can generate a report from the Compatibility task pane. Click Generate HTML Report in the Compatibility task pane, and Expression Web generates a new page and reports the errors. This report is a valuable tool when you're redesigning or analyzing a site. You can save or print this report for your own records or for your customer.

Key Points

- Expression Web helps you maintain W3C standards for validity.
- Expression Web helps you check and address accessibility issues.
- Using cascading style sheets helps keep your page uniform and provides easy access to an entire site's presentation.
- Using the correct DOCTYPE is a key to a valid, accessible page.
- You can add browsers and configure the Preview menu options in Expression Web.

Chapter at a Glance

Use tables for layout, **page 70**

Use lists to group information, **page 72**

Use semantic markup, **page 80**

Style the presentation of your content, **page 84**

4 Presenting Information on a Web Page

In this chapter, you will learn to:

✔ Use tables for layout.

✔ Use lists to group information.

✔ Use semantic markup.

✔ Style the presentation of your content.

At their most basic level, Web pages show information to visitors. Although this appears to be a simple concept, the modern Web adds some complexity. Page design should include considerations for accessibility regarding browsing devices of varied capability, for *search engines*, for *best practices*, and for *maintainability*.

Though it's beyond the scope of this book to provide a full-depth compendium on accessibility and search engine friendliness, the following exercises will help you form a good base of understanding of these considerations.

In this chapter, you will learn to use *tables* effectively on your Web page, and you will also learn to use *lists*. Then, you will learn to use *semantic markup*; and, finally, you will learn to style the presentation of the content on your page.

Important Before you can use the practice files in this chapter, you need to install them from the book's companion CD to their default location. See "Using the Book's CD" on page xiii for more information.

Troubleshooting Graphics and operating system–related instructions in this book reflect the Windows Vista user interface. If your computer is running Windows XP and you experience trouble following the instructions as written, please refer to the "Information for Readers Running Windows XP" section at the beginning of this book.

Using Tables for Layout: Right or Wrong?

Now that Web developers are consistently using cascading style sheets for layout, check any of the templates that came with Expression Web. You won't find a single one that uses a table for *layout*. The big question seems to be whether it's still acceptable to use tables. The answer is a definite Yes. Tables seem to have fallen out of favor for laying out pages; however, there are still plenty of good reasons to use tables, the most obvious of which is to present data in clear, *tabular* form.

In this exercise, you will use a properly coded and valid table structure to display some tabular data on your Web page.

> **USE** the *CH4* sample site. This site is located in the *Documents\Microsoft Press\Expression Web SBS\Sample Sites* folder.
>
> **BE SURE TO** start Expression Web before beginning this exercise.
>
> **OPEN** the *CH4* site, and display the *contact* page.

1. On the **View** menu, point to **Visual Aids**, and then click **Show**. Ensure that **Block Selection** is the only selected visual aid.

   Visual Aids can help you see the various elements in a table.

2. In the Design pane, set the insertion point at the end of the ZIP Code in the address, and then press [Enter] to create a new paragraph.

3. On the **Table** menu, click **Insert Table**. In the **Insert Table** dialog box, configure the table to have two *rows* and three *columns*, and accept the default settings.

4. Click **OK** to insert the table. In the upper-left table *cell*, type **Name**. Tab to the next cell and type **Email.** Tab to the next cell, and type **Phone**. Press ⌜Tab⌝ again to move the cursor to the first cell in the next row. Type a name, e-mail address, and phone number into the cells in the second row.

5. On the **View** menu, point to **Visual Aids**, and then click **Visible Borders** and **Empty Containers**.

6. After you type a phone number in the last cell of the second row, press ⟦Tab⟧ to create a new, third row. Type a name, e-mail address, and phone number into the cells in this row.

7. Save the page, and preview it in a browser to make sure that the page appears as you want.

 CLOSE the *contact* page.

Using Lists to Group Information

Among the essential tags for laying out information on a Web page are lists. There are three basic types of list, as shown in the following table.

List type	Tag	Purpose
Ordered list	*<ol>*	Numbered items
Unordered list	*<ul>*	Bulleted items
Definition list	*<dl>*	Term and definition arrangement

In this exercise, you will learn to insert all three types of lists and arrange information within them.

USE the *CH4* sample site. This site is located in the *Documents\Microsoft Press\Expression Web SBS\Sample Sites* folder.

OPEN the *CH4* site and display the *about_me* page.

Bullets

1. In the Design pane, set the cursor immediately after **Heading 2**, and press [Enter] to create a new paragraph. Type **Benefits** as a title for the list that will follow. Press [Enter] to create another paragraph, and type **First Benefit**. On the toolbar, click **Bullets**.

In Split view, notice that the <p> tag that previously surrounded the words *First Benefit* is now a <ul> tag, and the words are now wrapped in an <li> tag. The paragraph became an ***unordered list***, and the text became a ***list item***.

Increase Indent Position

2. Press [Enter] again to create a new list item line, and type **Second Benefit**. Press [Enter] once more to advance to the next list line; but before you type anything, click the **Increase Indent Position** button.

In the page code, notice that a <ul> tag appears within the preceding <li> tag; there is now a list within a list.

3. Type three items here, pressing [Enter] between them, so that there will be three items in this inner list.

Decrease Indent Position

4. When you reach the final list items in this inner list, click the **Decrease Indent Position** button.

In **Split** view, notice that the code for the inner list and list element was closed and you're back out in the original list you inserted.

5. Type two more entries: **Third Benefit** and **Fourth Benefit**, pressing [Enter] between them to set them each as list items. After you type **Fourth Benefit**, press [Enter] twice to end the list and create a new paragraph.

6. Save your page, and preview it in a browser to make sure that it appears as you want, and then switch to Expression Web.

7. In the Design pane, type **Instructions** in the paragraph immediately below your newly finished unordered list, and press [Enter] to create a new paragraph.

In this list example, we'll list instructions because they lend themselves by nature to an ordered, step-by-step type of list.

8. Type **First Step**, and then click **Numbering**.

Numbering

In Split view, notice that the <p> tag that previously surrounded the words *First Step* is now an <ol> tag, and the words themselves are now wrapped in an <li> tag. The paragraph is now an ***ordered list***, and the text is a list item.

9. Press ⌷Enter⌷ to create a new list item line, and type **Second Step**. Press ⌷Enter⌷ once more to create one more list item line, but before you type anything, click the **Increase Indent Position** button.

In the page code, notice the <ol> tag within the preceding <li> tag. There is again a list within a list.

10. Type three items here, pressing ⌷Enter⌷ between them.

11. When you reach the final item in this inner list, click the **Decrease Indent Position** button.

```
52        </ul>
53        </li>
54        <li>Third Benefit</li>
55        <li>Fourth Benefit</li>
56     </ul>
57     <p>Instructions</p>
58     <ol>
59        <li>First Step</li>
60        <li>Second Step<ol>
61           <li>Sub Step</li>
62           <li>Sub Step</li>
63           <li>Sub Step</li>
64        </ol>
65        </li>
66     </ol>
67     <p>Cras rutrum laoreet wisi. Pellentesque lorem. Sed commodo feugiat
```

In Split view, notice that Expression Web has closed the inner list and its final item, and returned to your original list.

12. Type two more entries: **Third Step** and **Fourth Step**, pressing ⌷Enter⌷ between them to set them each as list items. After you type **Fourth Step**, press ⌷Enter⌷ twice to end the list and create a new paragraph.

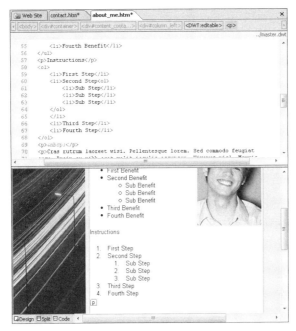

13. Save the page and preview it in a browser to make sure that it appears as you want, and switch to the Expression Web interface.

Definition lists are much less commonly used than numbered and bulleted lists but are valuable for lists of terms and their definitions.

14. In the paragraph below the other lists, type **Definitions**, and press [Enter] to create a
new paragraph. Type **First Term**. There is no button on the toolbar for **Definition**
lists, so click the paragraph tag in the quick tag selector bar that contains *First Term*
to select the entire tag. Click the drop-down arrow on the **Paragraph** style box on
the toolbar, and select **Defined Term <dt>**.

As in the other list examples, the <p> tag has been replaced by a <dl> tag, and
First Term is wrapped in a list item, this time a <dt> tag.

15. Press [Enter] to create a new line, which will be wrapped in a <dd> tag, and type a
few sentences to describe *First Term*. Press [Enter] again to create a new line.

You are now set up for another <dd> definition for *First Term*.

```
        </li>
        <li>Third Step</li>
        <li>Fourth Step</li>
    </ol>
    <p>Definitions</p>
    <dl>
        <dt>First Term</dt>
        <dd>This is a sentence describing the term above.  It&#39;s
        wrapped in a &lt;dd&gt; tag.</dd>
        <dd>This is a secondary definition of the term above.  It&#39;s
        also wrapped in a &lt;dd&gt; tag.</dd>
    </dl>
    <p>Cras rutrum laoreet wisi. Pellentesque lorem. Sed commodo feugiat
    arcu. Proin eu nibh eget velit iaculis accumsan. Vivamus nisl. Mauris
    sed risus. Vestibulum pede arcu, posuere eget, tincidunt in, porta vitae,
    dolor.</p>
```

Notice that the Definition list functions slightly differently than the other two types of list. A Definition list provides an easy way to supply multiple definitions for a single term.

16. Type a secondary definition in this new line, and press [Enter] once more.

At this point, we want to add a term, not a definition on this new blank line.

17. In the Code pane, change the **<dd>** and **</dd>** tags to **<dt>** and **</dt>** tags.

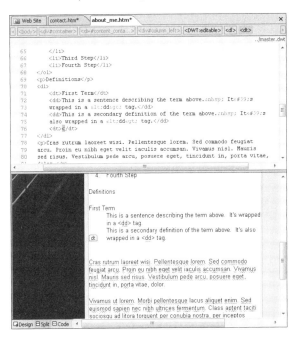

18. Type **Second Term**.

Notice how the new term lines up under the first term.

19. Press `Enter` to create a definition for this second term. Repeat this process a few times to become familiar with it. When you're done adding terms and definitions, press `Enter` twice to end the definition list and insert a new paragraph.

20. Preview the page in a browser to make sure that it appears as you want, and switch to the Expression Web interface.

 CLOSE the *about_me* page.

Using Semantic Markup

Rather than thinking of HTML elements as ways to style your text, think of them as ways to describe what the text means and use cascading style sheets to style their appearance.

For instance, a list by nature groups similar elements together in a way that several paragraphs don't. An H1 element shows more importance than the same words marked up with a large font size, and an <em> (emphasized) or a <strong> tag adds additional meaning to a word where a <b> (bold) tag simply changes the font but doesn't add to the word's perceived importance.

In this exercise, you will learn to use HTML elements to enhance the meaning of the text and cascading style sheets to modify the appearance of the elements.

USE the *CH4* sample site. This site is located in the *Documents\Microsoft Press\Expression Web SBS\Sample Sites* folder.

OPEN the *CH4* site and display the *contact* page.

1. In the Design pane, scroll to the table of employee contact data.

2. Select the top row of the table (the row that contains the words *Name, Email*, and *Phone*). In the Code pane, edit each of those table cell tags by replacing the **<td>** and **</td>** tags with **<th>** and **</th>**.

Notice how the Design view of the text that is contained in the cells changes slightly. This change occurred because you replaced a nondescript table cell with a *Table Head* cell. This tag indicates to search engines and non-visual browsers that this bit of data is different and is a heading for the columns below it.

Bold

3. Open the *about_me* page from the *about_me* folder. In the Design pane, click in the word *Benefits*, which is being used as a title for your list of benefits, and then click **Bold**.

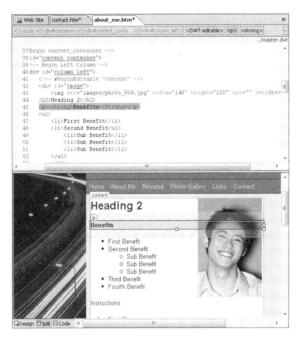

Notice that the page code now has the addition of a <strong> tag. This is much better than the old way: a <b> (bold) tag. Bold describes the look of the text, but Strong does more to describe its meaning.

4. Repeat step 3 for the word *Instructions*.

Italic

5. Click in the final list name, **Definitions**. This time, instead of using the Bold button to wrap the word in a <strong> tag, click the **Italic** button.

Notice that instead of the <i> tag for italic, the word is wrapped in an <em> tag, which means *emphasized*. The idea is that emphasized *means* something; italic only describes a font style.

 CLOSE the *contact* and *about_me* pages.

The value of this shift from presentational markup (font tags, italic tags, bold tags, and so on) to semantic markup is clear. The old way simply applied a visual appearance to the text; the new way does something to lend a bit of description, which assists search engines and non-visual browsers to understand a level of meaning that font tag markup can't supply.

Styling the Presentation of Your Content

In the preceding exercises, we put some lists and tables on the page. They definitely serve the purposes for which they were intended: they contain the information they were designed to contain, and they keep it segregated from other information. Semantically, lists and tables are superior to using paragraph tags or one paragraph with line breaks between the relevant blocks. The only problem with them is their appearance.

This is another case of cascading style sheets to the rescue. You will now learn how to maintain the semantic value of these tags for search engines and non-visual browsers, but style them so that they look appealing to visitors.

In this exercise, you will learn to style the presentation of your content by using a class and by styling the base HTML element.

USE the *CH4* sample site. This site is located in the *Documents\Microsoft Press\Expression Web SBS\Sample Sites* folder.

OPEN the *CH4* site and display the *contact* page.

1. On the **View** menu, click **Visual Aids**, and then click **Margins and Padding**.

2. In the Design pane, scroll to the employee contact table, and select the table row that contains the table heads (<th>).

3. In the **Apply Styles** task pane, click **New Style**. In the **New Style** dialog box, name the style **.tablehead**. Then select the **Apply new style to document selection** setting.

4. In the **Define in** box, click **Existing style sheet (../styles/style3.css)**.

5. Under **Font**, set **font-family** to **Courier New, Courier, monospace**; **color** to **#FFFFFF**; and **font-weight** to **bold**. Under **Block**, set **text-align** to **left**, and under **Background**, set **background-color** to **#000000**.

6. Click **OK** to close the dialog box.

> **Note** In the Style Builder/Modify Style dialog box, when you make a specification within a category, the category title is bold.

You've modified the appearance of all of the <th> elements within that row by adding a style class (*class="tablehead"*) to the <tr> tag that contains them.

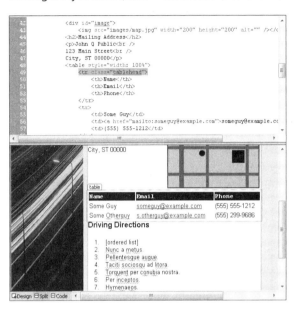

7. In the sample site, open the *about_me.htm* page from the *about_me* folder, and in the Code pane, select the **<ul>** tag below *Benefits*.

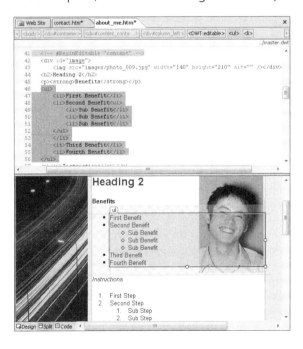

8. In the **Apply Styles task** pane, click **New Style**. In the **New Style** dialog box, name the style **.benefitlist**. Then select the **Apply new style to document selection** setting.

9. In the **Define in** box, click **Existing style sheet (../styles/style3.css)**.

10. Under **List**, set **list-style-type** to **square**. Then click **Apply**.

Notice that the outer <li> elements have a square bullet instead of the typical round bullet. Notice also that the inner list items still have a round bullet.

11. Change the *Selector* name from *.benefitlist* to **.benefitlist li**, and then click **Apply**.

Cascading Style Sheets

When using cascading style sheets, several methods of altering the presentation of HTML elements are available, including the following:

- ● **CSS ID**: In the style sheet code, it will always begin with a number symbol (#). IDs are designed to be used only once in a page and as such are generally used for major page elements such as DIVs that make up major portions of a page.

- ● **CSS Class**: In the style sheet code, it will always begin with a period (.) and can be used multiple times in a page if necessary.

You can also specify a style for a basic HTML element itself, such as an ordered list or an anchor tag. This can be particularly useful because you define the HTML element only once on your style sheet, and every time that element appears in a page, it will be styled in accordance with the style sheet's specification.

The dialog box title changes from New Style to Modify Style.

Notice that the inner list items now have a square bullet instead of a round bullet. This is because you classed the *<ul>* tag as *.benefitlist* but also added the *<li>* tag to that style specification in step 5. This procedure will produce an identical effect for both elements.

12. Click **OK** to close the **Modify Style** dialog box.

13. On the quick tag selector, select the **Instructions <ol>** tag, and in the **Apply Styles** task pane, click **New Style**. In the **New Style** dialog box, name the style **.instructionlist**. Then select the **Apply new style to document selection** setting.

14. In the **Define in** box, click **Existing style sheet (../styles/style3.css)**.

15. Under **List**, set **list-style-type** to **upper-roman**. Then click **OK** to close the **New Style** dialog box.

16. So that the inner list items do not have the same formatting as the parent element, in the **Apply Styles** task pane, right-click **.instructionlist**, and then click **New Style Copy**.

17. Give the new style the name **.instructionlist li li**, and under **List**, change **list-style-type** to **lower-alpha**. Then click **OK**.

Notice that the inner list items now show lowercase alphabetic list items, and the outer list items are uppercase roman numerals. Notice also that the only code that has been added to the page is the containing <ol> tag now has a class (*class="instructionlist"*) applied to it.

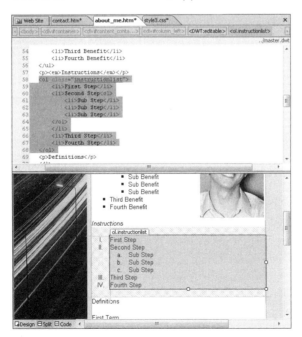

Another way to style an element is to style its basic HTML container.

18. In the **Apply Styles** task pane, click **New Style**, and type **dt** for **Selector**. Under **Font**, set **font-family** to **Courier New, Courier, monospace**; **font-weight** to **bold**; and **text-transform** to **upper case**.

Notice that the Definition list terms are now in all capital letters and are in Courier bold font.

19. In the **Apply Styles** task pane, click **New Style**, and add a **Selector** of **dd**. Under **Font**, set **font-family** to **Times New Roman, Times, serif**; **font-size** to **small**; and **color** value to **#808080**. Then click **OK**.

Notice that the definitions are now smaller and colored grey. These effects will apply to all Definition list terms and definitions in any page that has this style sheet linked to it. Notice also that the code in the page hasn't changed at all. This style is applied to all Definition list items by default without the need to class them or mark them separately. This feature is a great advantage if you should want to change the appearance of a styled HTML element; all you would need to do is change its entry on the style sheet, and every instance of that element in dozens, hundreds, or even thousands of pages would instantly change!

CLOSE the *CH4* sample site. If you are not continuing directly to the next chapter, exit Expression Web.

What is the real value of all this? Well, let's consider the worst-case scenario: you didn't use the list elements or the style sheet and classes to create these segments of information. You would have extensive *font tags* describing the appearance of every line, you would need to resort to paragraph indents and perhaps *block quotes* where they didn't even belong, and the file size of your code would be many times greater than it is now.

The best-case scenario: you've contained your information in a semantically valid element that adds to the meaning of the text itself, and you've given it the appearance that you want by creating styles on an external style sheet. You've prevented using a large amount of code, and you've given the text additional meaning beyond what can be seen. As a tremendous added bonus, an externally linked style sheet will be downloaded by the browser just once, cached, and used on any page that's linked to it. So, in addition to being cleaner and leaner, the code is also more efficient. Though this small example isn't as telling as a large site would be, the fact remains that these techniques can save space on your server, save page-load time for your site visitors, and add to content searchability.

Key Points

- Although using tables for layout is no longer a current best practice, tables still can be used effectively for tabular data.

- Lists are a cornerstone of displaying related information on Web pages.

- You can mark up your text as well as its semantic meaning.

- By using cascading style sheets to style text, you can gain easier maintenance of presentation while also reducing the overall code in the page itself.

- You can use cascading style sheet classes to style parent elements, copy classes to style inner elements, and even specify the default look of an HTML element through Expression Web's cascading style sheet tools.

- Using cascading style sheets to style elements by selector or by their basic HTML container greatly aids in the efficiency of keeping a site uniform and changing the appearance of items globally.

Chapter at a Glance

Use images as backgrounds, **page 106**

Add images to a Web page, **page 94**

Use images as bullets, **page 114**

Use images as hyperlink backgrounds, **page 116**

5 Enhancing a Web Site with Images

In this chapter, you will learn to:

✔ Add images to a Web page.

✔ Edit images in Expression Web.

✔ Use images with a style sheet.

✔ Use images as backgrounds.

✔ Use images as bullets.

✔ Use images as hyperlink backgrounds.

It goes without saying that a Web page is quite uninteresting without images. There-fore, ensuring that the images on your site display as expected is an important part of designing your site. Whether you use images to show a product, to convey a thought, or simply to enhance the page's aesthetic appearance, you're going to be using them in your pages. You don't want to use a bunch of large-size images that don't have any *alt text* or semantic value on a page.

In this chapter, you'll learn how to use images in your pages by using current best prac-tices, and you'll learn how to edit images in Microsoft Expression Web. You will learn some new ways to use images in conjunction with CSS to yield results that would otherwise be impossible or at the very least quite cumbersome. You'll learn how to use images in back-ground areas and to use images as bullets. Then, you will learn to use images as hyperlink backgrounds.

> **Tip** To view the formatting marks and provide visual layout cues for this chapter, on the View menu, click Formatting Marks, and then click Show.

Important Before you can use the practice files in this chapter, you need to install them from the book's companion CD to their default location. See "Using the Book's CD" on page xiii for more information.

Troubleshooting Graphics and operating system–related instructions in this book reflect the Windows Vista user interface. If your computer is running Windows XP and you experience trouble following the instructions as written, please refer to the "Information for Readers Running Windows XP" section at the beginning of this book.

Adding Images to a Web Page

Although putting images on a Web page may appear trivial at its core, there are key principles of modern Web design that you should understand to ensure the site you build is fast loading, accessible, and meaningful to search engines. Key considerations are page file size and accessibility. Although images will "show" what you want, they don't do anything to "tell" their story or add to the value of the information they're re-lated to. By understanding how to use images on a page correctly, you can universally enhance the point you're trying to make, providing impact, as well as making sure your image is accessible and search-engine friendly.

In this exercise, you will add a basic image to a Web page.

USE the *CH5* sample site. This site is located in the *Documents\Microsoft Press\Expression Web SBS\Sample Sites* folder.

BE SURE TO start Expression Web before beginning this exercise.

OPEN the *CH5* site.

1. In the **Folder List**, click the **images** folder of the sample site. On the **File** menu, point to **Import**, and then click **File**.

   The Import dialog box opens.

2. In the **Import** dialog box, click **Add File**, and browse to the *Documents\ Microsoft Press\Expression Web SBS\Files\CH5-Import* folder.

3. In the *Ch5-Import* folder, press [Ctrl]+[A] to select all of the files, and then click **Open**.

All the image file names appear in the Import dialog box.

4. Click **OK** to close the **Import** dialog box and import the pictures into your site's *images* folder.

5. In the **Folder List**, double-click the *default* page. Click just before the first letter of **Heading 2** in the content editable region. On the **Insert** menu, point to **Picture**, and then click **From File**.

The Picture dialog box opens.

> **Tip** In the Picture dialog box, you can click Views to choose one of several views: Thumbnails, Tiles, Icons, List, Details, Properties, or Preview. The most useful in Web design are Thumbnails and Preview.

6. In the *CH5\images* folder, click the *Pager* image, and then click **Insert** to close the dialog box.

The Accessibility Properties dialog box opens. This dialog box is intended to help you maintain your site's W3C validity and accessibility.

7. Enter a descriptive **Alternate text** value for the picture.

If you leave the text field blank, you will get an empty *alt* value (which is still valid but not descriptive).

8. Click **OK** to close the dialog box and insert the image.

> **Note** The entry for *Long Description* is there to allow you to browse to a text file with a verbose description of a complex image or if you want to provide long descriptions for images in order to provide greater accessibility to visually impaired visitors using a screen reader browser.

Although your picture is now in the page, it's not doing a very good job of enhancing the text that's adjacent to it.

9. Double-click the image to show the **Picture Properties** dialog box, and then click the **Appearance** tab. Under **Wrapping style**, click **Right**, and then click **OK**.

Your image has now floated to the right of the text.

Notice how your text comes into contact with the image's edge. This is less than ideal because it can make the text difficult to read and just doesn't look very good.

10. Double-click the image to open the **Picture Properties** dialog box. On the **Appearance** tab, type **5px** in the **Horizontal margin** box and in the **Vertical margin** box.

The image margin is now five pixels. The text no longer touches the image.

11. Save the page and preview it in a browser.

 BE SURE TO leave the *CH5* site open for use in the next exercise.

Consider the result of the previous lesson: You imported a folder full of images into your site's existing *images* folder, inserted an image into your page and styled it to be complementary to the page and text. All the while, Expression Web helped you maintain W3C validity and accessibility standards.

Editing Images in Expression Web

In general, a best practice is to prepare images in an *image editor*, such as Microsoft Expression Design, or whatever image editor you're partial to, before importing them into your site. The operations you'd do in the image editor would include adjustment of *physical size*, color adjustment, text overlay, and a host of other techniques, depending on the intended use of the image.

Although Expression Web isn't intended to be used as your image editor, it does contain a number of tools you can use to make quick adjustments. Any professional will have his or her preferred graphics tool for a given job, but the ability to make an adjustment to an image while creating a new layout or in the course of maintaining an existing site is a time-saving feature.

In this exercise, you will edit an image within Expression Web.

USE the *CH5* sample site you modified in the previous exercise.

OPEN the *CH5* site if it isn't already open.

1. On the *default* page, right-click the Pager image you inserted in the previous exercise, and then click **Show Pictures Toolbar**. Point to each button on the Pictures toolbar to view its tooltip.

Crop

2. On the **Pictures** toolbar, click **Crop**. Then drag the handles of the cropping box over the image to define the area of the image you want to keep.

3. Press Enter to crop the graphic. Then on the toolbar, click **Save**. In the **Save Embedded Files** dialog box, click **Rename**, and then change the image name to **PagerCrop.jpg** (to preserve the original image).

4. In the **Save Embedded Files** dialog box, click **OK**.

5. Double-click the image to open the **Picture Properties** dialog box, and then click **Edit**.

The image opens in a Microsoft Paint window.

> **Troubleshooting** If Microsoft Paint is not your default image editor, you can right-click the image and then click Open With to select the image editor of your choice.

Text

6. Click the **Text** button, and draw a text box at the bottom of the image. In the text box, type **Emergency Service**.

7. Save the picture as **PagerCropText.jpg**, and then close Paint.

8. On the *default* page, double-click the image to open the **Picture Properties** dialog box, and then click **Browse**. Navigate to the site's *images* folder, click the *PagerCropText* image, and click **Open**. Click **OK** to close the **Picture Properties** dialog box, and then save the page.

9. Click the bottom of the text paragraph in the **content** editable region, and then press ⌷ Enter ⌷ to insert a new paragraph.

10. Insert the *TestTubes* image that you imported into the site earlier in this exercise.

11. Double-click the image to show the **Picture Properties** dialog box, and then click **Picture File Type**.

In the Picture File Type dialog box, you can choose different file types: JPEG, GIF, and PNG. You can also change the image compression.

12. Clear the **Use image as is** check box, and change the **Quality** level to **60**.

The image file size has been reduced significantly. You can also set the number of Progressive Passes for the image in the box below the Quality box, but this is generally only needed for purposely high file–size images such as high-quality artwork samples.

13. Click **OK** in the **Picture File Type** dialog box, and then click **OK** in the **Picture Properties** dialog box. Save the page and accept the default settings on the **Save Embedded Files** dialog box.

BE SURE TO leave the *CH5* site open for use in the next exercise.

Important Be careful when compressing images, whether through the facilities in Expression Web or another image editor. As you compress them, the file size will get lower along with the quality. For optimum image compression, you're looking for a balance between file size reduction and acceptable appearance.

Using Images with a Style Sheet

With the advent of cascading style sheets (CSS), some capabilities that were previously unavailable or that required significant hand coding are now made easy through Expression Web's various CSS interfaces. In the upcoming exercise, you will manipulate an image's presentation by using CSS. Doing so will keep unnecessary code out of your page and make sure that the code that is there is modern, in keeping with W3C standards, and easily maintainable.

In this exercise, you will learn a few things that you can do with your style sheet and a simple image inserted into your page within the text content.

> **Important** In each of the following exercises, you will be adding and changing CSS code that's directly entered onto the page itself rather than on an attached style sheet. In each of the following exercises, make sure to select the Apply New Style To Document Selection check box and select Current Page for the Define In value.

> **USE** the *CH5* sample site you modified in the previous exercise.
>
> **BE SURE TO** enable Visual Aids for Block Selections, Visible Borders, and Margins And Padding before beginning this exercise.
>
> **OPEN** the *CH5* site if it isn't already open.

1. In Design view, click the page just before the first letter of the first paragraph in the **content** editable region.

2. On the **Insert** menu, point to **Picture**, and then click **From File**. In the **Picture** dialog box, navigate to the site's *images* folder, click the *chips* image, and then click **OK** to close the dialog box and insert the picture. Give the picture a meaningful **Alternate text** description when prompted.

3. In Design view, click the image you just inserted, and then click **New Style** in the **Apply Styles** task pane. Change the **Selector** name to **.chippic**, and then specify the following settings:

Category	Option	Value
	Apply new style to document selection	Selected
Box	padding	10px (Same for all selected)
Layout	float	left

4. Click **OK** to close the dialog box and create your new style.

5. In the **Apply Styles** task pane, right-click **.chippic**, and then click **Modify Style**. In the **Category** list, click **Layout**, and then change **float** to **right** to see an alternative to the initial setting. Click **OK** to save your changes and close the **Modify Style** dialog box. Review your changes in Design view.

> **Note** To find the style for an item more easily, select it in your page, and then in the Apply Styles task pane, click Options, and then click Show Styles Used On Selection.

6. Click the image again in Design view. Right-click its style in the **Apply Styles** task pane, and then click **Modify Style** to open the **Modify Style** dialog box. Click **Layout** in the **Category** list again, and then in the **cursor** box, click **help**. Click **OK** to close the dialog box and return to Design view. Save your page and preview it in a browser.

7. With the page open in your browser, point to the image you just worked on.

The cursor changes to a *Help cursor* (question mark and pointer).

This technique of specifying the cursor for an image element can be helpful in giving your visitor a visual cue that there's additional information available about an image via its alt text that will pop up when hovered over.

8. Switch to Expression Web and display Split view. Click the image you just styled in the **Design** pane, and look at its representation in the **Code** pane. Notice that there isn't any code added to the image tag other than *class="chippic"*.

9. Press ⌷Ctrl, and then in the **Code** pane, click the underlined style.

This is known as a *code hyperlink* and it will focus your editor on that style and show the style in question as highlighted.

```
    padding: 10px;
}
body {
    padding: 0px;
    margin: 0px;
}
.chippic {
    padding: 10px;
    float: right;
    cursor: help;
}
</style>
</head>

<body>
```

 BE SURE TO leave the *CH5* site open for use in the next exercise.

Consider what you accomplished in this exercise; using just the style sheet facilities in Expression Web, you modified the layout of a picture on the page and caused it to show the visitor a different cursor when it's hovered over, and all of this without writing any code by hand.

Using Images as Backgrounds

One of the best things about using CSS and images together is the ability to use the images as backgrounds. You can use CSS to style background images in tables and table cells, but for maximum flexibility, you can use CSS to style the background images by using DIV elements.

The flexibility to repeat or not repeat (generally known as *tiling*), keep the image as a static background so that it doesn't scroll with the page elements, and even layer images over each other are simply not things you can accomplish through any other method.

Expression Web contains some of the best CSS interface tools ever available to a designer. Through Expression Web's various panels and interfaces, you can not only take advantage of the benefits of CSS and images to style backgrounds with minimal learning required, if you have an interest in digging deeper under the hood of how CSS works, you can simply see the code results in the attached CSS file or embedded styles that occurred from your actions within the Expression Web interface.

In this exercise, you will learn to use images as backgrounds on various page areas.

USE the *CH5* sample site you modified in the previous exercise.
OPEN the *CH5* site if it isn't already open, and display the *Backgrounds* page in Split view.

1. In the **Code** pane, click the <div> tag containing *class="top"*. In the **Apply Styles** task pane, right-click **.top**, and then click **Modify Style**.

2. In the **Modify Style** dialog box, click **Background** in the **Category** list, then click **Browse** beside the **background-image** box. Navigate to the site's *images* folder, double-click the *BGtop* image, and click **no-repeat** in the **background-repeat** list. Then click **OK** to close the dialog box and return to your page.

You've just specified a background image for the top div by using the interface.

3. In the **Code** pane, click the <div> tag (*class="left"*) below where you were just working. In the **Apply Styles** task pane, right-click **.left**, and then click **Modify Style**. Repeat step 2 to insert the *BGleft* image.

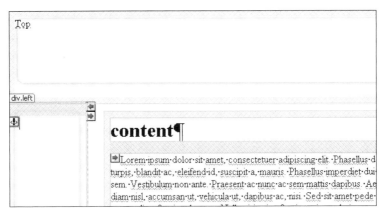

4. In the **Code** pane, click the <div> tag (*class="foot"*) at the bottom of the page. In the **Apply Styles** task pane, right-click **.foot**, and then click **Modify Style**. Repeat step 2 to insert the *BGfoot* image.

5. In the **Code** pane, click the <div> tag (*class="content"*) that contains the main content. In the **Apply Styles** task pane, right-click **.content**, and then click **Modify Style**. Navigate to the site's *images* folder, double-click the *BGcontent* image, but don't set any other values. Click **OK** to close the dialog box and return to your page. Save the page and preview it in a browser.

Notice that tiles of the image you just specified fill the entire area of the DIV element.

6. In the **Code** pane, click the content <div> tag again. In the **Apply Styles** task pane, right-click **.content**, and then click **Modify Style**. Click **Background** in the **Category** list, click **no-repeat** in the **background-repeat** list, click **center** in the **(x) background-position** list, and then click **center** in the **(y) background-position** list.

7. Click **OK** to save your changes and close the dialog box. Save your page and preview it in a browser. Notice that your background image shows only once.

8. Take this *watermark* background situation a little farther and make the following modifications to the style: In the **Code** pane, click the content <div> tag. In the **Apply Styles** task pane, right-click **.content**, and then click Modify Style. Specify the following settings:

Category	Option	Value
Position	height	300px
Layout	overflow	auto
Background	background-attachment	fixed

9. Click **OK** to close the dialog box and return to your page. Save the page and preview it in a browser.

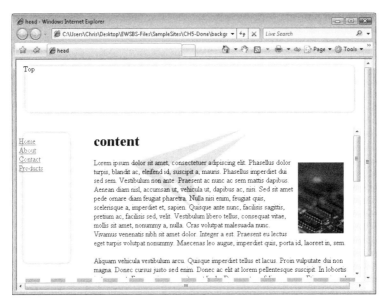

Notice how your background image now stays static within the page and the text scrolls over it. It's looking more like a watermark background.

To use the CSS background image property for more than just showing an image, consider the previous exercise where you added text to an image by using Paint from within Expression Web. It showed text over a picture but that's about it, plus it wasn't something that a search engine would pick up or that a screen reading browser would be able to read.

10. In the **Code** pane, click just to the left of the <h1> tag in the content DIV element, type the following code, and then press Enter:

```
<div><p>Emergency Service</p></div>
```

11. In the **Design** pane, click this newly inserted DIV element, and then click **New Style** in the **Apply Styles** task pane:

12. In the **New Style** dialog box, change the **Selector** to **.emgsvc**, and then specify the following settings:

Category	Option	Value
	Define in	Current page
	Apply new style to document selection	Selected
Background	background-image	BGPagerCrop.jpg
	background-repeat	no-repeat
Position	width	129px
	height	156px
Layout	float	right

13. Click **OK** to save your changes and return to Design view in Expression Web.

> **Tip** In order to make design easier, try this: create a new Web page, and save it in your *images* folder. Select all the images in the folder, and then drag them onto the page. The page now displays all the images, providing a visual cue as to which image is which. Expression Web enters the dimensions of each image in its image tag.

14. Save the page, and preview it in a browser.

You've now got an image in your page via a styled background, and you've got text on top of it.

15. To make your text appear similar to the exercise in Paint, return to Expression Web, click the paragraph inside the *.emgsvc* DIV element that contains the words *Emergency Service*, and then click **New Style** in the **Apply Styles** task pane. Type **.emgtxt** in the **Selector** box, specify the following settings, and then click **OK** to close the dialog box:

Category	Option	Value
Font	font-size	13px
	font-weight	Bold
	color	#FF0000
Background	background-color	#FFFFFF
Box	margin top	143px (**Same for all** check box cleared)

16. Save the page and preview it in a browser.

Notice that you've got a very close representation of the image you edited in an earlier exercise, but this time its actual text within your page, not just an image of text superimposed on a picture.

 BE SURE TO leave the *CH5* site open for use in the next exercise.

Although this exercise got you started with how to style background images and how to manipulate the background's property, it's not intended to be a treatise on CSS. You can do so much with CSS that entire books could be, and have been, written on the subject and even then they're forced to leave out some details. I highly recommend taking time to learn about CSS and how you can really maximize its impact on how you design your pages.

Using Images as Bullets

Although there are a number of default bullet styles you can specify through CSS, sometimes you want to style a page in such a way as to take total control of the appearance of the bullets. Without CSS, you would have to resort to using paragraphs with positioned images, laying out a table to contain the images used for bullets, or both. In any case, you lose the semantic value of your list elements and load up your page with unnecessary markup. Using CSS, specifying images in an unordered list is a surprisingly simple matter.

In this exercise, you will substitute images for default bullets in a standards-compliant, semantically valid, easily maintainable way, and using very limited code.

USE the *CH5* sample site you modified in the previous exercise.

OPEN the *CH5* site if it isn't already open, and display the *Backgrounds* page in Split view.

1. Select the unordered list in the content by clicking its representation on the quick tag selector bar.

2. In the **Apply Styles** task pane, click **New Style**.

3. Create a new style called **.notelist**, and select the **Apply new style to document selection** check box, but don't set any other properties. Then click **OK**.

4. In the **Apply Styles** task pane, right-click **.notelist**, and then click **New Style Copy**. Give this copy the name **.notelist li**.

5. Click **List** in the **Category** list, click **Browse** next to the **list-style-image** box, navigate to the site's *images* folder, and double-click the *li* image. Then click **OK**.

6. In the **Apply Styles** task pane, click **OK**.

Notice that you've now got a musical note for all the list item elements.

7. In the **Apply Styles** task pane, right-click **.notelist li**, and then click **New Style Copy**. Give this new copy the name **.notelist li li**.

8. Click **List** in the **Category** list, click **Browse** next to the **list-style-image** box, navigate to the site's *images* folder, and double-click the *lili* image. Then click **OK**.

9. Save the page and preview it in a browser.

Notice that the inner list elements have a different list item image.

 BE SURE TO leave the *CH5* site open for use in the next exercise.

Styling an unordered list by using CSS by using Expression Web's interface is remarkably easy. Consider the visual impact you can make with little more than a few images and a couple of clicks, as you did in the previous exercise.

Using Images as Hyperlink Backgrounds

Using images as hyperlinks has long been a staple of Web design; the individual images serve as buttons, and combined within a page area, they serve as navigation bars. A designer might use JavaScript to make the images display a *roll-over* effect. Expression Web's Interactive Buttons feature makes it easy to create buttons like this by using images and JavaScript.

In this exercise, you will create an alternative to these buttons with nothing more than a regular text-based hyperlink, two images, and a little CSS, with *no JavaScript at all.*

USE the *CH5* sample site you modified in the previous exercise.

OPEN the *CH5* site if it isn't already open, and display the *Backgrounds* page in Split view.

1. In the **Code** pane, click just under the style block describing the **.left** style.

2. Paste or type the following code into your page.

```
.left a {
    width: 100px;
    height: 30px;
    display: block;
    background-image: url('images/BGlink.jpg');
    background-repeat: no-repeat;
    text-align: center;
    text-decoration: none;
    color: white;
    font-weight: bolder;
    font-size: 15px;
    padding-top: 5px;
    margin-left: 11px;
}
```

Note Any code you need to enter in this lesson is available in a .css file that you imported into your site's *images* folder earlier in this chapter.

```
}
.left a {
    width: 100px;
    height: 30px;
    display: block;
    background-image: url('images/BGlink.jpg');
    background-repeat: no-repeat;
    text-align: center;
    text-decoration: none;
    color: white;
    font-weight: bolder;
    font-size: 15px;
    padding-top: 5px;
    margin-left: 11px;
}
```

3. Save your page and preview it in a browser.

Notice that you've got a pretty nice arrangement that looks like a button. The only thing you don't have is the *image swap* feature common to graphic buttons.

4. Switch to Expression Web. In Code view, or in the **Code** pane of Split view, type the following code just below the block you entered in the previous step:

```
.left a:hover {
    background-image: url('images/BGlinkOver.jpg');
}
```

5. Save your page and preview it in a browser. Point to the links and notice the image swap effect they now have.

This is a very flexible technique, and, when compared to a JavaScript-based image button, is much better from the perspective of accessibility and ease of maintenance.

6. To wrap up this exercise and see how these style changes appear in Expression Web's style builder, right-click **.left a** in the **Manage Styles** task pane, and then click **Modify Style** to show the **Modify Style** dialog box.

On the left of the dialog box, in the Category list heading, every category that has a modification made to it will be in bold. You can click each of these modified category entries to see how these changes you entered directly into the page code are represented within the dialog box.

CLOSE the *CH5* sample site and any open Internet Explorer windows. If you are not continuing directly to the next chapter, exit Expression Web.

Key Points

- Use images properly in your pages, being sure to avoid excessive page file size and download time without adding any descriptive value to the content.
- Expression Web has tools to make rudimentary image editing possible from within the Expression Web interface.
- If you use CSS and a background image, you achieve the same results visually as you would by using an edited image, and you also gain additional semantic value, search-engine friendliness, and accessibility.
- By using Expression Web's interface, you can easily replace default bullets with custom images.
- By using CSS, you can create CSS-only image buttons that have a roll-over effect, minimizing page size and improving semantic value and accessibility.

Chapter at a Glance

Create a template-based site, **page 122**

Modify a site's Dynamic Web Template, **page 129**

Modify a site's cascading style sheet, **page 135**

6 Creating a Web Site from a Template

In this chapter, you will learn to:

✔ Create a template-based site.

✔ Organize Web site pages.

✔ Modify a site's Dynamic Web Template.

✔ Modify a site's cascading style sheet.

Creating a Web site from an empty folder is a daunting challenge for all but the smallest of sites. Fortunately, Microsoft Expression Web comes with a collection of pre-installed *Web site templates* that you can use to get a head start on the process of creating a site. In these site templates, you'll find valid HTML code, and layouts that use cascading style sheets rather than tables for positioning. Each site relies on a Dynamic Web Template to control page layout and presentation. What you won't find are proprietary features, unattractive *clip art*, discouragingly deep table structure, or any of a multitude of issues that plagued Expression Web's predecessors.

The pre-installed templates are organized in three groups: Organization, Personal, and Small Business. The organization is related more to the *architecture* of the templates (number of pages and page names) than to their actual purposes—so regardless of the purpose of the site you are building, consider all of the templates and find the one that best suits your aesthetic interests. It's easier to add or remove pages from a template-based site than it is to make major changes to the visual presentation of the site.

Templates such as those provided by Expression Web aren't only a good way to get a quick start on your site project; they're also a good way to learn (by doing) about elements such as Dynamic Web Templates, cascading style sheet layouts, and general Expression Web skills.

In this chapter, you will first learn about choosing a template that best suits the site you want to build. Then you'll learn how to modify a template-based site by organizing its pages, modifying its Dynamic Web Template, and modifying its cascading style sheet files.

> **Important** Before you can use the practice files in this chapter, you need to install them from the book's companion CD to their default location. See "Using the Book's CD" on page xiii for more information.

> **Troubleshooting** Graphics and operating system–related instructions in this book reflect the Windows Vista user interface. If your computer is running Windows XP and you experience trouble following the instructions as written, please refer to the "Information for Readers Running Windows XP" section at the beginning of this book.

Creating a Template-Based Site

As you approach the task of creating a new Web site based on one of the templates that Expression Web provides, you'll be wise to first have an idea of what you want the outcome to look like, and to then look at each of the templates with an eye toward finding the one that most closely represents the look you're seeking.

In this exercise, you will choose one of the supplied templates and create a new site from it.

> **BE SURE TO** start Expression Web before beginning this exercise. If Expression Web opens a previous site, click Close Site on the File menu.

1. On the **File** menu, point to **New**, and then click **Web Site**.

   The New dialog box opens, displaying the Web Site tab.

2. On the left side of the **New** dialog box, click **Templates**.

   The installed templates appear in the center pane of the dialog box.

3. Click each template to see a description and *thumbnail* view of the site in the pane on the right side of the dialog box.

4. Examine each template, and then click the **Organization 5** template.

5. In the **New** dialog box, click **Browse**, and then navigate to the *Documents/ My Web Sites* folder.

   You will create the template-based site in this folder.

6. In the **New Web Site Location** dialog box displaying the contents of the *My Web Sites* folder, click the **New Folder** button, and then create a folder named **CH6**.

7. In the **New Web Site Location** dialog box, click **Open**.

   The New Web Site Location dialog box displays the selected location.

8. Click **OK**.

   Expression Web creates and opens a site based on the Organization 5 template.

9. In the **Folder List**, double-click the *default.htm* page to have a closer look at what you've just created.

Because the Web site templates that come with Expression Web rely on Dynamic Web Templates, an active cursor appears on only the content section of the page. Any changes you want to make to the template itself will be done by directly editing the Dynamic Web Template.

10. Preview this new page in a browser to see what it looks like as a visitor would encounter it, and be sure to click the links to the other pages within the site and examine them.

11. Close the browser window and return to Expression Web.

By this time, you should have a good idea of what pages are created with the template you selected, and which pages you want to keep, which pages you need to delete, and whether you need to add any pages that don't already exist.

 BE SURE TO leave the *CH6* site open for use in later exercises.

Organizing Web Site Pages

After creating a site based on a template, as you did in the previous exercise, the first task you should undertake is organizing the pages. This task includes creating pages you need that don't yet exist, deleting pages you don't need, and organizing the folder locations and properties of existing pages.

In this exercise, you will delete the photo gallery and information links folders and the pages they contain, modify the properties of existing pages, and add a folder and a page.

 USE the *CH6* site you created in the previous exercise.
OPEN the *CH6* site if it isn't already open.

1. Click the **Web Site** tab at the top of the workspace to switch to Web Site view.

2. In the **Folder List**, right-click the *photo_gallery* folder, and then click **Delete**. In the **Confirm Delete** dialog box, click **Yes**. Repeat this step for the *information_links* folder.

3. In the **Folder List**, double-click the *about* folder to expose the page within.

The page is named *about.htm*.

4. Right-click *about.htm*, click **Rename**, and then rename the page *default.htm*. In the **Confirm Rename** dialog box asking whether you want to update all linked pages, click **Yes**.

5. Right-click the newly renamed *default.htm* page, and then click **Properties**.

6. In the **default.htm Properties** dialog box, change the original, and less than descriptive, *document title* from "About" to something like "About *site name*" or "About *business name*."

> **Tip** You can optimize search engine results by including the name of the business, person, or organization in the page title.

7. In the **Properties** dialog box, click **OK**.

8. Repeat steps 3 through 7 to rename the main page within each of the following folders to **default.htm**, and then change the page title.

Folder	File
calendar	calendar.htm
contact	contact.htm
faq	faq.htm
news	news.htm

When you finish, each of the five folders (about, calendar, contact, faq, and news), as well as the root folder, will contain a file named *default.htm*.

Next, you will create another folder and page within the site.

New Document

9. In the **Folder List**, click the root folder. On the toolbar, click the **New Document** arrow, and then click **Folder**.

Expression Web creates a folder named *New_Folder* and selects the folder name so you can change it.

10. Type **products**, and then press ⌨Enter.

To display content when a site visitor links to the *products* folder, you need to create an ***index file*** within it.

11. Select the newly created *products* folder, and then on the toolbar, click the **New Document** button.

Expression Web creates a blank Web page named *Untitled_1.htm*.

Save

12. On the toolbar, click **Save**.

13. In the **Save As** dialog box, navigate to the *products* folder. In the **File name** box, enter **default.htm**.

14. In the **Save As** dialog box, click **Save**.

15. In the **Folder List**, double-click the *products* folder, right-click the *default.htm* file it contains, and then click **Properties**. Rename the page with a meaningful name, and then click **OK** to close the dialog box.

Notice that this page bears no resemblance to any of the other pages in this site. This is because this page is not attached to the Dynamic Web Template.

16. On the **Format** menu, point to **Dynamic Web Template**, and then click **Attach Dynamic Web Template**.

17. In the **Attach Dynamic Web Template** dialog box, browse to the site's *master.dwt* Dynamic Web Template, and select it.

18. Click **OK** to close the dialog box and attach the template to your new page.

Your newly created page now has the correct template applied to it and is identical in style and layout to all the other pages in the site.

BE SURE TO leave the *CH6* site open for use in later exercises.

You have just seen the big benefit of using Dynamic Web Templates to control layout of Web pages: There's virtually no chance that pages attached to a Dynamic Web Template can have an inconsistent appearance, not to mention the ease of maintaining *global elements* such as navigation, which you'll tackle in the next exercise.

Modifying a Site's Dynamic Web Template

All of the templates that are provided by Expression Web use a Dynamic Web Template. There's a reason: it's virtually a necessity for today's Web site designer to use some sort of **templating system**, whether it's an ASP.NET **master page** arrangement, a Dynamic Web Template, or some other form of **server-side** template. Prior to the arrival of Expression Web, Web editing software used proprietary themes, shared borders, and all kinds of convoluted mechanisms to control page layout and presentation across a Web site. The Dynamic Web Template capabilities that are available through Expression Web are still a "save time" feature, because the templating takes place on your local computer before your site is published to the server; so no proprietary server capabilities are required.

In this exercise, you will modify the Dynamic Web Template to reflect the navigational changes you made in the earlier exercises, you will add a link for the products page you created, and you will then add a logo to the top of the page.

> **USE** the *CH6* site you modified in the previous exercise.
>
> **OPEN** the *CH6* site if it isn't already open.

1. In the **Folder List**, double-click **master.dwt** in your site's root folder to open it for editing within Expression Web.

2. In Design view, in the left navigation section of the page, click **Photo Gallery**.

   Look at the quick tag selector bar and notice that you're inside not only an <a> tag, but you're also inside an <li> list element because the navigation for this template is actually an unordered list.

3. In the quick tag selector bar, click **<li>** to select the <a> tag and the <li> tag that contains it. Press Del to remove the link.

4. Repeat steps 2 and 3 for the list item and the link for the page titled *Links*.

   The two pages that you deleted are now removed from the navigation. Next, you will add a link for your new Products page.

5. In the Design pane, click just after the last letter in the word **Home** in the navigation section of the page, and then press Enter to break to a new line and create a new <li> tag. Type **Products**, select the word you just typed, right-click, and then click **Hyperlink**. In the **Insert Hyperlink** dialog box, browse to the *products* folder, and then click the **default.htm** file.

6. Click **OK** in the **Insert Hyperlink** dialog box to close it and set the link.

7. In the Design pane, click the bottom of the page just before the *pipe character* (|) that follows the entry for **Links**. Select back to and including the pipe character that follows the entry for **Calendar**, and then press [Del] to clear the removed pages from the lower link bar.

8. Click just after the pipe character that follows the entry for **Home**, press [Space], type **Products**, add another space, and then insert another pipe character (|).

9. Select the word **Products**, being careful not to also include any empty spaces, right-click **Products**, and then click **Hyperlink**. In the **Insert Hyperlink** dialog box, browse to the *products* folder, and then click the **default.htm** file.

10. Click **OK** to close the dialog box and set the link.

11. In the **Folder List**, click the **images** folder. On the **File** menu, point to **Import**, and then click **File**.

12. In the **Import** dialog box, click **Add File**. In the **Add File to Import List** dialog box, navigate to the *Documents\Microsoft Press\Expression Web SBS\Files* folder, select *logo.jpg* and *BGlogo.jpg*, and then click **Open** to add these images to the files list.

13. Click **OK** to import these images into your site's *images* folder.

14. In Design view, click the very beginning of the H1 element that contains **Organization**. On the **Insert** menu, point to **Picture**, and then click **From File**.

15. In the **Picture** dialog box, locate the *images* folder, click **logo.jpg**, and then click **Insert**. When you are prompted, give the image some descriptive alternate text, and then click **OK** to close the dialog box and insert the image.

Notice that your logo image is centered, along with the H1 element that contains it.

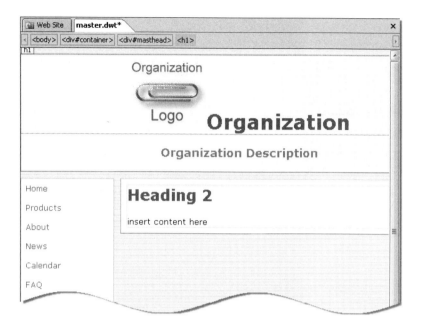

16. Right-click the image, and then click **Picture Properties**. On the **Appearance** tab, change the **Wrapping Style** to **Left**, and then click **OK** to close the dialog box.

Your logo image now floats to the left of the text elements within the top banner of your page.

17. Save the page. In the dialog box that opens, asking if you want to update all the pages linked to the Dynamic Web Template, click **Yes**.

18. Open the **default.htm** page from the root folder, and preview it in a browser. Check your links and layout to make sure that your changes to the Dynamic Web Template are present in the pages that the template is attached to.

 BE SURE TO leave the *CH6* site open for use in later exercises.

Obviously, if this exercise were the actual creation of a site, you would be working on other elements such as changing the text of the headings in the top banner, possibly adding graphics or other elements to the left navigation area, and other modifications that would be necessary for a real Web site. You should now be comfortable with working in a Dynamic Web Template to the extent that you will continue with the tasks that are needed to design a professional-looking Web site.

> **Troubleshooting** If you modify a site's Dynamic Web Template, and the attached pages don't update, try this: On the Site menu, click Recalculate Hyperlinks. If that doesn't remedy the situation, open all the pages in the site that are attached to the Dynamic Web Template, make a trivial change to the Dynamic Web Template, such as add a space, and then remove the change you just made. When you save the Dynamic Web Template, all the open pages should get updated. Then, click Save All on the File menu.

Modifying a Site's Cascading Style Sheets

As a wrap-up of the presentational work you started by modifying the Dynamic Web Template in the previous exercise, you will likely want to make some changes to colors, backgrounds, and other presentational elements of the template, which are controlled by the site's cascading style sheets.

In this exercise, you will modify the background of the top banner in order to provide a more visually appealing logo. You will change the behavior of the links in the lower navigation bar, and you'll experiment with the additional style sheets you will find within the site template's styles folder that are provided by Expression Web.

USE the *CH6* site you modified in the previous exercise.

OPEN the *CH6* site if it isn't already open, and then display the *master.dwt* file located at the root of the site.

1. On the **Format** menu, point to **CSS Styles**, and then click **Manage Style Sheet Links**.

   The Link Style Sheet dialog box opens.

2. By default, this site's Dynamic Web Template is linked to *style2.css* in the *styles* subfolder. Click **styles/style2.css**, and then click **Remove**. Next, click **Add**, navigate to the *styles* folder, and then click the *style1.css* file. Click **OK** to close the dialog box and switch to your page.

3. Save the Dynamic Web Template, accept its updates to attached pages, and then preview in a browser the *default.htm* file from the root folder.

Notice the radical change that is present in the page visually.

It's amazing that you can change the entire presentation of every page in a Web site without changing one single line of HTML code in the pages.

4. Close the browser window and switch to Expression Web. Repeat steps 2 and 3. However, this time, attach *style3.css*.

5. After you've examined the site when it has *style3.css* attached, close the browser, switch to Expression Web, and change the style sheet back to the *style2.css* file that was originally attached.

> **Tip** Every one of the templates that come with Expression Web contains multiple style sheets. When you use one of these templates, make sure to check these alternate style sheets. They'll always be in the *styles* folder. If you're interested in seeing what other site developers can do with a style sheet, look at *www.csszengarden.com*. There, you'll find a single HTML file and dozens of user-submitted cascading style sheet files that style the HTML file. Some of the cascading style sheet files are incredible, but they all exhibit the variety of design effects style sheets can have on HTML files.

6. In Design view, click the logo image that you inserted in the previous exercise, and press ⌦. On the quick tag selector bar, click **<div#masthead>**.

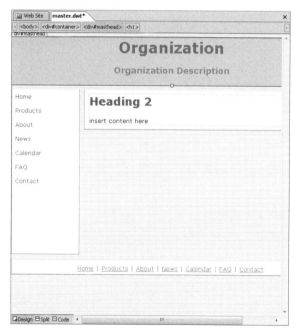

7. RIght-click the **<div#masthead>** entry in the **Manage Styles** task pane, and then click **Modify Style**.

The Modify Style dialog box opens.

8. In the **Category** list, click **Background**, and then change the **background-color** value from *#fafaff* to **#C0C0C0**. Next to the **background-image** box, click **Browse**, locate the *images* folder, and then double-click the *BGlogo.jpg* image. In the **background-repeat** list, click **no-repeat**. In the **(x) background-position** list, click **left**.

9. In the **Category** list, click **Position**. Type **115px** into the **height** box, and then click **OK** to save your changes and close the dialog box.

10. Save the *master.dwt* file.

You will be prompted with the Save Embedded Files dialog box.

11. Accept the default **Overwrite** action, and click **OK** to save the file and close the dialog box.

12. When you are asked whether to save the changes to all the files in the site that this Dynamic Web Template is attached to, click **Yes**.

13. Preview the *default.htm* page from the root folder in a browser, and look at the presentation of the top banner.

Notice that a logo has floated to the left and has a gradient that blends into the DIV element's background color on the right. Notice also that the header elements are not skewed to the right as they were in the example in the previous exercise.

14. Close the browser window and switch to Expression Web.

15. In Split view, click one of the links at the bottom of the site's Dynamic Web Template. Look at the quick tag selector bar, and notice that an <a> tag is inside a <div#footer> tag.

16. Look in the **Manage Styles** task pane on the lower right of the workspace. Right-click the entry for **#footer a:hover**, and then click **Modify Style**.

17. In the **Modify Style** dialog box, click **Font** in the **Category** list.

Notice that the None check box is selected under text-decoration.

18. Select the **underline** and **overline** check boxes, which automatically clears the **none** check box.

19. Click **OK** to change the style and close the dialog box.

20. Return to the Dynamic Web Template, and click one of the links in the footer again. In the **Manage Styles** task pane, right-click **#footer a**, and then click **Modify Style**.

Notice that the Underline check box is selected under text-decoration.

21. Select the **none** check box, click **OK** to save and close the dialog box, and then save the Dynamic Web Template. At the prompt in the **Save Embedded Files** dialog box, accept the default settings to save the file.

22. Preview the *default.htm* page from the root folder in a browser, and review your work. Notice the rollover effect on the lower navigation bar.

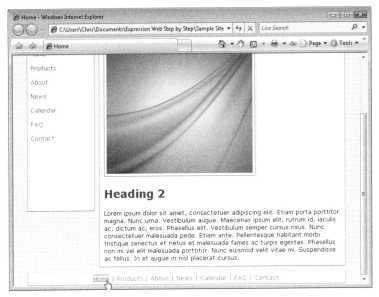

Now the links show no underline by default, and when you point to them, they show an underline and overline.

 CLOSE the *CH6* Web site and any open Internet Explorer windows. If you are not continuing directly to the next chapter, exit Expression Web.

Key Points

- Expression Web provides a number of Web site templates that you can use.
- Each template contains multiple style sheets, each giving the site a distinctively different appearance.
- Dynamic Web Templates are used in each of Expression Web's site templates.
- Sweeping changes can be made on every page in a Web site by simply modifying the Dynamic Web Template.
- Changes to a Dynamic Web Template will be automatically applied to all pages the template is attached to.
- Modifying the cascading style sheets file for a site template causes all pages in the site to reflect those changes.

Chapter at a Glance

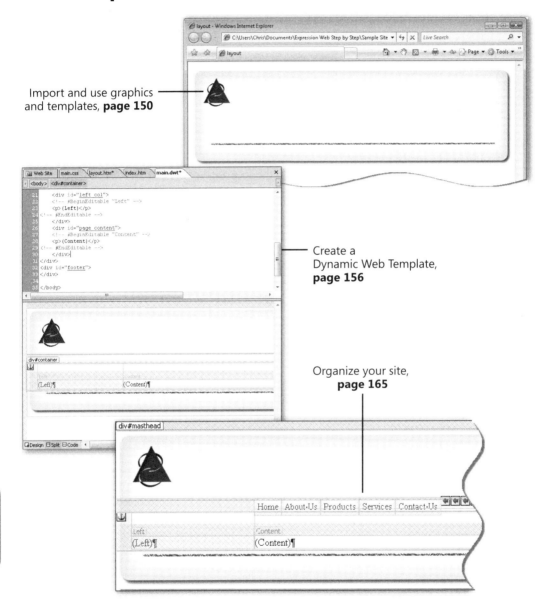

Import and use graphics and templates, **page 150**

Create a Dynamic Web Template, **page 156**

Organize your site, **page 165**

7 Creating a Web Site from Scratch

In this chapter, you will learn to:

✔ Create an empty site.

✔ Import and use graphics and templates.

✔ Create a Dynamic Web Template.

✔ Create content pages.

✔ Organize your site.

Starting a site from scratch is usually done when a designer has already designed the underlying graphics for the pages and is ready to translate the graphic elements into an HTML document. A designer sets up these graphics in a graphics editing application such as Microsoft Expression Design, Adobe Photoshop, Adobe Fireworks, Corel PaintShop Pro, or any other graphics application. In addition to designing the overall page graphics, the designer will *slice* the graphics, which results in multiple pieces of the original graphic that can be used in an HTML document as buttons, backgrounds, and various other graphic elements.

Another reason for starting a site from scratch might be that the designer purchased a template from an online outlet, such as Template Monster, Pixelmill, Classy Themes, or any of hundreds of other sites that sell Web site *template packages*.

Regardless of the reason for starting a Web site from scratch, the major work isn't in building the collection of pages that make up the site, but in developing that one single template page that all the other pages are based on.

Fortunately, Microsoft Expression Web has all the tools that you need to start with an empty site and end up with a valid and accessible HTML template.

In this chapter, you will learn how to create an empty site, how to import and use graphics and templates, and how to create a Dynamic Web Template. You will learn to create content pages, and then you'll learn how to organize your site.

Important Before you can use the practice files in this chapter, you need to install them from the book's companion CD to their default location. See "Using the Book's CD" on page xiii for more information.

Troubleshooting Graphics and operating system–related instructions in this book reflect the Windows Vista user interface. If your computer is running Windows XP and you experience trouble following the instructions as written, please refer to the "Information for Readers Running Windows XP" section at the beginning of this book.

Creating an Empty Site

The first step in creating a site from scratch is to create a container for all the pages, folders, and images that will eventually reside within the site. Sometimes called a *root folder*, in Expression Web this container is called a *site*, and it generally contains metadata that allows Expression Web to keep track of various site details, including what pages the site contains, how the pages link to each other, when each file was last modified, and where the Web site has been published to. An empty site is much more than just an empty folder.

Note To change Expression Web's default behavior of opening with the last site you worked on, on the Tools menu, click Application Options, and then on the General tab, clear the Open Last Web Site Automatically When Expression Web Starts check box.

In this exercise, you will create an empty site and a page to serve as a template.

 BE SURE TO start Expression Web before beginning this exercise. If Expression Web opens a previous site, click Close Site on the File menu.

1. On the **File** menu, point to **New**, and then click **Web Site**. In the middle of the **New** dialog box, click **Empty Web Site**.

2. Click the **Browse** button to the right of the **Location** box. Navigate to the *Documents/My Web Sites* folder. Create a folder named **CH7** for the new site, and then click **Open**.

You return to the New dialog box, and the location you just created appears in the Location box.

3. Click **OK** to create the site and close the dialog box.

You now have a newly created, empty site open in Expression Web. The first thing you need to do for your new site is create a folder to contain your graphics.

4. In the **New Document** list, click **Folder**. Name this newly created folder **images**.

This folder will serve as a container for all of the images you will use in your site.

The next thing you need is a page that you can use to start creating a template. You could start a Dynamic Web Template at this point, but it's easier to create a layout on a regular page, and then transfer that content over to a Dynamic Web Template later.

5. In the **New Document** list, click **Page**. On the **Page** tab of the **New** dialog box, click **CSS layouts**, click **Header, nav, 2 columns, footer** (the fifth layout in the CSS layout list).

6. In the **New** dialog box, click **OK** to create the page.

7. On the toolbar, click **Save**. In the **Save As** dialog box, type **layout** in the **File name** box, and then click **Change Title**. In the **Set Page Title** dialog box, type **layout** in the **Page title** box.

8. Click **OK** in the **Set Page Title** dialog box, and again in the **Save As** dialog box.

You are prompted to save the CSS file that was created along with the new page.

9. Name the CSS file **main**, and then click **Save**.

 BE SURE TO leave the *CH7* site open for use in the next exercise.

Visual Aids

When you create a page containing non-specific content such as DIV elements and styles, you will see visual representations of that content in Design view only if you display the visual aids.

When the visual aids are hidden, you see only a blank page.

To display visual aids:

→ Point to **Visual Aids** on the **View** menu, click **Show**, and select all of the **Show** options.

That wraps up creating an empty site and adding a file to serve as your initial template layout page. It's a fairly simple process, but performing it as in the preceding steps ensures that Expression Web will keep all of the files segregated from other folders and files on your hard disk. Expression Web will also establish metadata, so that the application can keep track of some behind-the-scenes details and make sure that file associations within the site will be kept up to date and accurate.

Importing and Using Graphics and Templates

To start laying out graphics and progressing in the next exercise, you need to get all the graphics and associated files into your site structure. Although there are a number of ways to bring these files into your site structure, many of them can be problematic. It's important to follow the examples and instructions in the following exercise. The best practices method that is presented in the next exercise will ensure that Expression Web recognizes what you're bringing in and can keep track of the locations of these files. Expression Web will also recognize the files' physical size, file size, and date of last modification, among other things.

In this exercise, you will import graphics and use them in an HTML page.

> **Important** For the following exercise, you need a graphics template. It can be from a commercial site such as one of those mentioned in the beginning of this chapter, or you can have one that you created yourself using your preferred graphics editor. Either way, graphics editors generally export your work under the same paradigm: they output an HTML file and sliced graphics to a folder.

> **USE** the *CH7* site that you created in the preceding exercise.
> **OPEN** the *CH7* site, if it isn't already open.

1. In the **Folder List**, click the root folder. On the **File** menu, point to **Import**, and then click **File**.

2. In the **Import** dialog box that opens, click **Add Folder**. In the **File Open** dialog box, navigate to the *Documents\Microsoft Press\Expression Web SBS\Files\CH7template* folder, and then click **Open**.

   The Import dialog box now displays all of the files inside the *CH7template* folder.

3. Click **OK** to import the folder and all of the files it contains.

4. In the **Folder List**, double-click the newly imported *CH7template* folder to expose the files it contains. Double-click the *index.htm* file within it and examine the layout.

> **Note** Although you cannot use this layout file for your template, it is valuable because you can use it to see what size the images are. You can also check the file size of the overall page in the lower-right corner of your design area. Split view is particularly helpful in this situation.

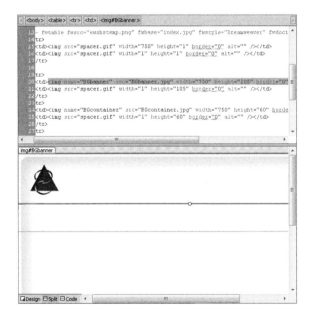

5. Open the *layout.htm* file that you created in the preceding exercise.

The first thing you need to do is appropriately style the *#container* DIV element.

6. In the *index.htm* file, locate *BGcontainer.jpg*. This graphic is 750 pixels wide and 60 pixels high. Switch to the *layout.htm* file, and on the quick tag selector bar, click **div#container**.

7. In the **CSS Properties** task pane, expand the **background** entry, click **background-image**, click the ellipsis button (**...**), and then click the *BGcontainer.jpg* file in the *CH7template* folder.

8. In the **CSS Properties** task pane, set the **background-repeat** value to **repeat-y**.

9. Change the **width** value to **750px**.

10. In *layout.htm*, select the top DIV element, which has the CSS ID **masthead**.

This DIV element will use the top image on the template page, *BGbanner.jpg*, which has a width of 750 pixels and a height of 105 pixels.

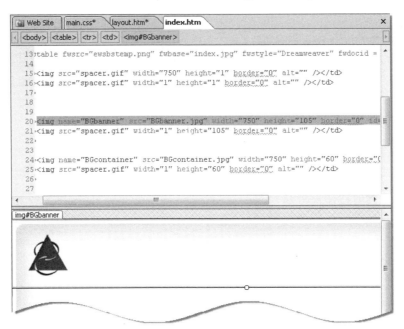

11. In the **CSS Properties** task pane, find the **background-image** entry, and then select *BGbanner.jpg*. Set the **background-repeat** value to **no-repeat**, the **height** to **105px**, and the **width** to **750px**.

12. In the **Code** pane, click the bottom DIV element. In the **CSS Properties** task pane, click the ellipsis button (…) for the **background-image** value, and then double-click the *BGbottom.jpg* file in the *CH7template* folder.

13. Set the **background-repeat** value to **no-repeat**, the **height** to **60px**, and the **width** to **750px**. Save the page, and preview it in a browser.

The key page areas now have appropriate background images, and what was once an empty page is now beginning to have the appearance of a "real" Web page.

14. Return to Expression Web, and then click the DIV element with a CSS ID of **top_nav**. In the **CSS Properties** task pane, click the ellipsis button (…) for the **background-image** value, and then double-click *BGcontainer.jpg* in the *CH7template* folder.

15. Set the **background-repeat** value of this DIV element to **no-repeat**, the **width** to **750px**, and the **height** to **20px**.

16. In the **Code** pane, click the DIV element with a CSS ID of **left_col**. In the **CSS Properties** task pane, change the **left** value from 0px to **25px**.

The DIV element moves to the right 25 pixels so that navigation or content in the DIV element will be clear of the shadow area at the edge of the container.

17. In the **Code** pane, click the DIV element with a CSS ID of **page_content**. In the **CSS Properties** task pane, change the **margin-left** value from **200px** to **225px** to make up for the movement of the adjacent **left_col** DIV element that you modified in step 15.

The previous steps conclude the process of inserting graphics into an HTML template as backgrounds for the DIV elements so that you can place content into them.

18. Save your page, and preview it in a browser for a final check.

CLOSE any open Internet Explorer windows.
BE SURE TO leave the *CH7* site open for use in the next exercise.

If you were actually creating a site, you'd still have work to do, such as styling the text that falls into the content area, designing and styling the links in the top navigation, and all kinds of other things. Taking you through each individual facet of CSS design is beyond the scope of this book, but you can easily use the lessons in previous chapters to enhance the design of this template. The preceding chapters contain examples of using cascading style sheets for navigation, content, lists, and other page elements.

Creating a Dynamic Web Template

When your general layout is done and your style sheet is able to present your layout and background as you want them, it's time to move the design to a Dynamic Web Template so that you can easily attach the design to any number of pages that you require. You'll also gain the benefit of updating the template in one single location, and of having those changes immediately affect all of the pages that are attached to the Dynamic Web Template.

In this exercise, you will create a Dynamic Web Template, move your layout design into it, and set up editable regions in both the visible Design view and the Code view (*HEAD* element).

USE the *CH7* site that you modified in the preceding exercise.
OPEN the *CH7* site if it isn't already open.

1. In the **Folder List**, click the root folder. In the **New Document** list, click **Page**.

The New dialog box opens.

2. In the **General** category on the **Page** tab, click **Dynamic Web Template**, and then click **OK** to create the Dynamic Web Template and close the dialog box.

A file named *Untitled_1.dwt* is now open in Expression Web. Notice that this page has one *<div>* tag and one editable region named *body*. You need to move the layout from your previous page (*layout.htm*) into this page and set up editable regions where you want them.

3. Open the *layout.htm* file, and then click **<body>** on the quick tag selector bar.

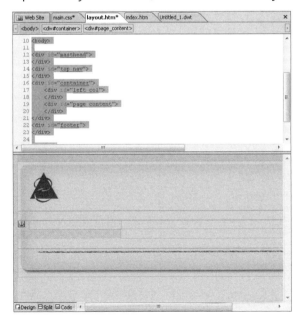

4. In the **Code** pane, right-click the highlighted code, and then click **Copy**.

5. Switch to the *Untitled_1.dwt* file, and then click **<body>** on the quick tag selector bar. In the **Code** pane, right-click the highlighted code, and then click **Paste**.

You've just transferred the layout of your original template page to this Dynamic Web Template. Notice that the Dynamic Web Template doesn't look at all like your original layout page. That's because it's not linked to the appropriate style sheet.

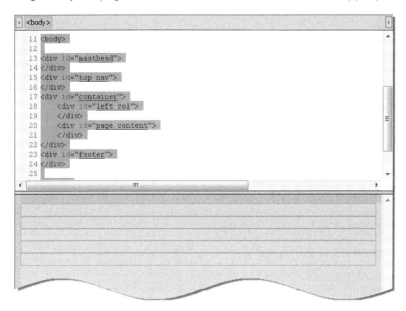

6. On the **Format** menu, point to **CSS Styles**, and then click **Attach Style Sheet**. In the **Attach Style Sheet** dialog box, click **Browse**, double-click the *main.css* file.

7. Click **OK** to attach the style sheet and close the dialog box.

Now your Dynamic Web Template looks identical to the layout page that you previously made.

8. On the toolbar, click **Save** to save your changes to the Dynamic Web Template. In the **Save As** dialog box, give the template a file name of **main**. Click **Change Title**, and change the title to **Template**.

9. Click **OK**, and then click **Save** to save the file and close the dialog box.

   Now that your Dynamic Web Template is set up to look like the template you had at the beginning of this exercise, you need to add some editable regions to it. Rather than start in the obvious places (div#left_col and div#page_content), you're going to set up an editable region in the HEAD element.

10. Set your Dynamic Web Template in **Split** view, and scroll to the top of the file.

    You'll see code that looks like this:

```
<head>
<meta http-equiv="Content-Type" content="text/html; charset=utf-8" />
<!-- #BeginEditable "doctitle" -->
<title>Template</title>
<!-- #EndEditable -->
<link rel="stylesheet" type="text/css" href="main.css" />
</head>
```

   As you can see, there's an editable region wrapped around the <title> element. This is in place so that each file you attach to the Dynamic Web Template can have its own unique title. It's a start, but it's not really enough.

11. Right-click the **Design** pane, and click **Page Properties**. In the **Page Properties** dialog box, in the **Page description** box, type **This is the description of this particular page**. Type some keywords into the **Keywords** box. It doesn't matter what you put there for now, but you should use comma-separated words, such as **keyword**, **keywords**, **other keywords**. Click **OK** to close the dialog box.

In the Code pane, the beginning of the Dynamic Web Template now looks like this:

```
<head>
<meta http-equiv="Content-Type" content="text/html; charset=utf-8" />
<!-- #BeginEditable "doctitle" -->
<title>Template</title>
<!-- #EndEditable -->
<meta name="keywords" content="keyword, keywords, other keywords" />
<meta name="description" content="This is the description of this particular
page" />
<link rel="stylesheet" type="text/css" href="main.css" />
</head>
```

12. To include the keywords and description meta elements into the editable region, select the line *<!-- #EndEditable -->*, right-click the highlighted text, and then click **Cut**. Click just after the closing angle bracket at the end of the description <meta> element, and press Enter to advance one line. Right-click, and click **Paste**.

The code now looks like this:

```
<head>
<meta http-equiv="Content-Type" content="text/html; charset=utf-8" />
<!-- #BeginEditable "doctitle" -->
<title>Template</title>
<meta name="keywords" content="keyword, keywords, other keywords" />
<meta name="description" content="This is the description of this particular
page" />
<!-- #EndEditable -->
<link rel="stylesheet" type="text/css" href="main.css" />
</head>
```

You have moved the close of the editable region to below the keywords and description <meta> tags, ensuring that they can be changed in all of the pages that attach to the Dynamic Web Template.

13. On the toolbar, click **Save** to save the changes to the *main.dwt* file.

The next regions you set can be done through the graphical user interface (GUI).

14. In the **Code** pane, click the **page_content** DIV element. On the **Format** menu, point to **Dynamic Web Template**, and then click **Manage Editable Regions**.

The Editable Regions dialog box opens.

15. In the **Editable Regions** dialog box, type **Content**. Click **Add** to create a new editable region, and then click **Close**.

16. In the **Code** pane, click the **left_col** DIV element. On the **Format** menu, point to **Dynamic Web Template**, and then click **Manage Editable Regions**. In the **Editable Regions** dialog box, name the region **Left**, click **Add**, and then click **Close**.

Notice how the Design pane now shows the name of the editable regions surrounded by parentheses where you set them.

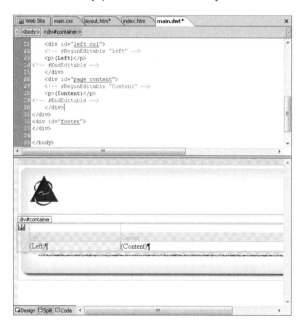

The editable regions are also surrounded by a <p> tag. This is the default behavior of Expression Web, but you can enter any text into these areas. For example, you might want to enter some instructional text for your end user, such as a paragraph or two about what kind of text to enter, or how to perform certain operations.

17. For now, leave the editable regions as they are, and save the *main.dwt* file.

 BE SURE TO leave the *CH7* site open for use in the next exercise.

In the preceding exercise, you created a usable Dynamic Web Template at its most basic level. You would normally work on other things also, such as entering and styling a heading for the company name in the #masthead section, and maybe adding a slogan to be visible beside it. You would certainly enter and style a menu in the #top_nav DIV element, and you'd add links to certain key pages and a copyright notice in the #footer DIV element. All of these tasks should be obvious, and most of them would be done after the additional pages are created. You'll find examples and exercises to provide deeper detail on these tasks in other chapters in this book.

Creating Content Pages

Two important reasons for using Dynamic Web Templates are:

- The ability to create new pages that carry the same template as all other pages in a site or group of pages.
- To enable end users to edit, enter, and change content on the pages without the possibility of damaging the template.

In this exercise, you will create new pages that are based on a Dynamic Web Template, and you'll edit these pages and their page properties.

 USE the *CH7* site you modified in the previous exercise.
OPEN the *CH7* site if it isn't already open.

1. In the **New Document** list, click **Create from Dynamic Web Template**. In the **Attach Dynamic Web Template** dialog box, click **main.dwt**.

2. In the **Attach Dynamic Web Template** dialog box, click **Open**.

Expression Web creates a new page named *Untitled_1.htm*.

3. On the toolbar, click **Save** to save the new page. In the **Save As** dialog box, type **default** into the **File name** box, and then click **Change Title**. In the **Set Page Title** dialog box, type **Home Page** in the **Page title** box, and then click **OK**. In the **Save As** dialog box, click **Save** to save the page and close the dialog box.

Notice that when you move the mouse pointer over the newly saved *default.htm* file, it takes the form of an insertion point only in those editable regions.

4. Right-click the **Design** pane, and then click **Page Properties**.

Notice that you can see the same keywords and description that you set up in the Dynamic Web Template earlier in this exercise.

5. Change the content of the **Page Description** and **Keywords** boxes to something that is appropriate for the page.

6. Click **OK** to close the **Page Properties** dialog box.

7. Repeat steps 1 to 6 to create some additional pages for your site. For this example, create the following pages: *about.htm*, *products.htm*, *services.htm*, *contact.htm*, and *legal.htm*.

> **Tip** You might find it faster to right-click the first page you created, click Copy, and then press Ctrl+V as many times as you need pages. Then, in Folders view, right-click the page, and click Rename. Open each page, right-click the Design pane, click Page Properties, and then change the content in the Title, Page Description, and Keywords boxes.

 BE SURE TO leave the *CH7* site open for use in the next exercise.

In the preceding exercise, you created enough pages to get your site project under way and to give you some pages to build menus for. This whole paradigm of a Dynamic Web Template to contain all of a site's common elements and content pages results in a powerful way to work. Not only can you keep end users from breaking your template, but you can also make it easy for users to work only in defined areas within pages.

You might have noticed that the Dynamic Web Template/Content Page arrangement is a very quick way to create a collection of pages. To go a step further, you could design a slightly different Dynamic Web Template for each section of a site, or multiple Dynamic Web Templates to provide different presentations. The Dynamic Web Template is also a great tool for a designer to use in order to show a client several different layouts, and when the client decides on a particular layout, it's a painless matter to build all of the necessary pages for the project based on the chosen template.

Organizing Your Site

Now that you have a collection of pages that are attached to a Dynamic Web Template, it's time to create some navigation to link them together and some basic text and links for the footer, and to clean up leftover pages and unnecessary files.

It's easier to keep unused files out of your site on an ongoing basis or at key milestones than it is to allow them to accumulate and then try to clean it all up at the end of the project.

In this exercise, you will create basic navigation, delete unnecessary pages, and organize your site.

> **USE** the *CH7* site that you modified in the previous exercise.
>
> **OPEN** the *CH7* site, if it isn't already open, and close any open pages.

1. Open the *main.dwt* file in **Split** view.

   To make a navigation bar for this site, we'll use an unordered list and place it in the top_nav DIV element of the *main.dwt* file.

2. In the **Design** pane, click the **top_nav** DIV element. On the toolbar, click **Bullets** to set an unordered list, and then type: **Home**, **About Us**, **Products**, **Services**, and **Contact Us**, pressing [Enter] between each to make each of these entries a new list item.

   Your page is going to look broken, because you're dropping an unordered list into a DIV element that's only supposed to be 20 pixels high; but you'll be using cascading style sheets in the next few steps to straighten it all out.

3. In the **Design** pane, for each of the list items you entered in the previous step, select the text, right-click the selected text, and click **Hyperlink**. Then in the **Insert Hyperlink** dialog box, click the appropriate page, and click **OK**.

   > **Tip** Double-clicking a word will select the entire word, and triple-clicking will select all of the words in a list item, or paragraph (such as About Us). In the Insert Hyperlink dialog box, double-clicking the page you want to link to will select that page and close the dialog box.

4. From the *Documents\Microsoft Press\Expression Web SBS\Files\Code* folder, open the *CH7CSS* text file, and copy its contents to the Clipboard. Switch to Expression Web and the *main.dwt* file. In the **Code** pane, find the underlined style ID **top_nav**, hold down the ⌈Ctrl⌉ key, and click **top_nav**.

```
<link rel="stylesheet" type="text/css" href="main.css" />
</head>

<body>

<div id="masthead">
</div>
<div id="top_nav">
<ul>
    <li><a href="default.htm">Home</a></li>
    <li><a href="about.htm">About Us</a></li>
    <li><a href="products.htm">Products</a></li>
    <li><a href="services.htm">Services</a></li>
    <li><a href="contact.htm">Contact Us</a></li>
</ul>
```

This is called a code hyperlink and the effect is that it will open the style sheet it's linked to with that particular class or ID highlighted.

```
/* CSS layout */
#masthead {
    background-image: url('CH7template/BGbanner.jpg');
    background-repeat: no-repeat;
    height: 105px;
    width: 750px;
}

#top_nav {
    width: 750px;
    height: 40px;
    background-repeat: no-repeat;
    background-image: url('CH7template/BGcontainer.jpg');
}

#container {
    position: relative;
    width: 750px;
    background-image: url('CH7template/BGcontainer.jpg');
    background-repeat: repeat-y;
    height: 60px;
}

#left_col {
    width: 200px;
    position: absolute;
    left: 25px;
    top: 0px;
}

#page_content {
    margin-left: 225px;
}

#footer {
    background-image: url('CH7template/BGbottom.jpg');
    background-repeat: no-repeat;
    height: 60px;
    width: 750px;
}
```

5. Right-click the highlighted code, click **Paste,** and then save the CSS file. Switch to *main.dwt* and notice the changes to the navigation bar.

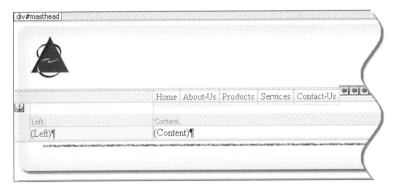

> **Note** Rather than running through one more exercise on building cascading style sheets in Expression Web, you can simply copy and paste the code from the sample disk. If you're interested in seeing what happens in the Expression Web interface, you can use the Manage Styles task pane to explore it within the Modify Styles dialog box.

6. Click the **#footer** DIV element in the template. In the **Manage Styles** task pane, right-click **#footer**, and then click **Modify Style**. In the **Modify Style** dialog box, under the **Font** category, give the **font-size** a value of **x-small**, click the swatch next to **color**, pick up the eyedropper tool, select the burgundy color in the logo of your Dynamic Web Template, and then click **OK**.

The Modify Style dialog box opens.

7. In the **Category** list, click **Block**. Set the **text-align** value to **center**.

8. In the **Category** list, click **Box**. Clear the **Same for all** check box for the **padding**, and then set the **top** value to **20**.

9. Click **OK** to close the dialog box and save your changes.

10. In the **Design** pane, type a copyright statement such as **Copyright 2007 SampleSite, 123 Any Street, Some Town, Some State. All rights reserved** into the **footer** DIV element in your *main.dwt* file.

11. Select the entire line that you typed in the previous step, right-click the highlighted text, click **Hyperlink**, click *legal.htm*, and then click **OK** to close the **Insert Hyperlink** dialog box.

    Notice that when you set your hyperlink on that line of text, it loses its burgundy color and becomes the default blue of a normal hyperlink.

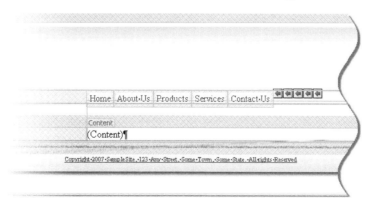

12. In the **Manage Styles** task pane, click **New Style**. In the **New Style** dialog box, give the **Selector** a value of **#footer a**. In the **Font** category, give the **color** entry a value of **#810101**, and then click **OK** to close the dialog box.

13. Save your page. When prompted, allow the CSS file to save, overwrite, and allow the Dynamic Web Template to update all the pages it's attached to.

14. Preview *default.htm* in a browser and check your work. Click the navigation links and footer link to make sure they're all correct.

15. Switch to Expression Web, and expand the *CH7template* folder in the **Folder List** that you imported earlier in this set of exercises. Hold down the ⌨ key, and click the three files you used: *BGbanner.jpg*, *BGbottom.jpg*, and *BGcontainer.jpg*. Drag these files to the **images** folder in the **Folder List**.

Expression Web updates the references to those files throughout the site and in the CSS file.

16. On the **Site** menu, point to **Reports**, and then click **Site Summary**. Click **Unlinked Files**, and delete each of these unlinked and unnecessary files.

17. In the **Folder List**, delete the *CH7template* folder because it's now empty and also unnecessary.

That wraps up the organization of your site template.

CLOSE the *CH7* Web site, any open Internet Explorer windows, and the *CH7CSS.txt* file. If you are not continuing directly to the next chapter, exit Expression Web.

This chapter and its exercises provided you with a foundation for how to make a template in Expression Web. There are many fine points that you'll need to know, or need to learn, in order to produce professional-level work—that's not the purpose of this book. As you become comfortable with the general concepts that are outlined in this book, you should also learn the basics of cascading style sheets and many other techniques that, when combined, can be used to enable you to create top-level professional designs.

Key Points

- You can import any Web site template into an Expression Web site and use it to create a Dynamic Web Template.

- Expression Web contains a number of CSS page layouts that you can use to get a head start on creating a template.

- Editable regions can exist in both Design view and the code elements of a Dynamic Web Template.

- You can identify and remove unused files by using Reports view.

- Dragging and dropping files will update any instance of their use throughout your site.

Chapter at a Glance

Use interactive buttons, **page 174**

Use layers and behaviors, **page 181**

Create and use forms, **page 192**

Use Personal Web Packages, **page 188**

8 Taking It to the Next Level

In this chapter, you will learn to:

✔ Use interactive buttons.

✔ Use layers and behaviors.

✔ Use Personal Web Packages.

✔ Create and use forms.

Beyond simply showing text, images, and other media on your pages, you can use the features in Microsoft Expression Web to do more with *static pages* and provide your site visitors with a more interactive experience. By using these features, you'll be able to add both visual and functional elements to your pages.

In this chapter, you'll learn to use interactive buttons, layers, behaviors, Personal Web Packages, and forms to create interesting effects and functionality.

Important Before you can use the practice files in this chapter, you need to install them from the book's companion CD to their default location. See "Using the Book's CD" on page xiii for more information.

Troubleshooting Graphics and operating system–related instructions in this book reflect the Windows Vista user interface. If your computer is running Windows XP and you experience trouble following the instructions as written, please refer to the "Information for Readers Running Windows XP" section at the beginning of this book.

Using Interactive Buttons

Link bars, which are made up of a series of buttons, and even individual link buttons have long been a staple of Web site navigation. Previously, you would have to create the images to use for these buttons, often in multiple "***states***," and then create some JavaScript code to animate them and give them a "roll-over" effect. Even if you used the cascading style sheets–only method from Chapter 5, "Enhancing Your Web Site with Images," you'd still need to create the images.

Expression Web provides a nice feature for adding these buttons to a page without the need to create images, JavaScript, or even cascading style sheets (CSS). The feature is called *Interactive Buttons*. There are more than 220 different styles and colors available for you to insert into your pages.

Here's a scenario: in your site, you need to add an area that contains links to other "partner" sites that are similar in nature to the one you're working on. This link area needs to be on every page in your site. You don't want plain links; instead, you want buttons.

> **Tip** Because you need these link buttons on every page in this site, you can easily make use of the Dynamic Web Template to provide this functionality and to make maintaining these links very easy.

In this exercise, you will use the Interactive Buttons feature to create a group of links in all of the pages in your site.

USE the *CH8* sample site. This site is located in the *Documents\Microsoft Press\Expression Web SBS\Sample Sites* folder.

BE SURE TO start Expression Web before beginning this exercise.

OPEN the *CH8* site, and then display the *master.dwt* file in Split view.

1. On the **View** menu, click **Visual Aids**, and then click **Block Selection**.

2. In the **Design** pane, click **Headline 3**.

Notice the editable region.

3. Because you want this group of links to be present on all pages but not editable by other users working on those pages, click in the **Code** pane just before the following line:

```
<!-- #BeginEditable "sidebar" -->
```

and then type **Great Resources**.

```
    <!-- #BeginEditable "content" -->
    <h2>Headline 2</h2>
    <p>insert content here</p>
    <!-- #EndEditable --></div>
<!-- End Left Column -->
<!-- Begin Right Column -->
<div id="column right">
Great Resources
    <!-- #BeginEditable "sidebar" -->
    <h3>Headline 3</h3>
    <p>insert content here</p>
    <!-- #EndEditable --></div>
<!-- End Right Column -->
<!-- Begin Footer -->
<div id="footer">
    <div id="copyright">
```

4. In the **Design** pane, click the line you just typed. On the toolbar, click the **Style** arrow, and then click **Heading 3 <h3>**. Click at the end of the H3 element, and then press ⎵Enter⎵ to insert a new paragraph.

5. On the **Insert** menu, click **Interactive Button**.

The Interactive Buttons dialog box opens, with the Button tab selected.

6. In the **Buttons** list, click **Embossed Capsule 6**. In the **Text** box, type **Expression Web**; in the **Link** box, type **http://by-expression.com**.

7. Click the **Font** tab, and notice the settings that you can change. For this example, leave the defaults in place, and click the **Image** tab.

> **Note** The Image tab contains options to size the button, specify what image states are created, and whether they should be preloaded. Below these options are more, important options to create a *JPEG* image and specify a background color, or to create a *GIF* image that has a *transparent background*.

8. For the best-looking result, use a JPEG image, click the color list, and then click
More Colors to show the **More Colors** dialog box. Click **Select**, and then click the
Design pane of your page to pick up the background color of the area where you'll
be placing the Interactive Button (*Hex={CC,BB,99}*).

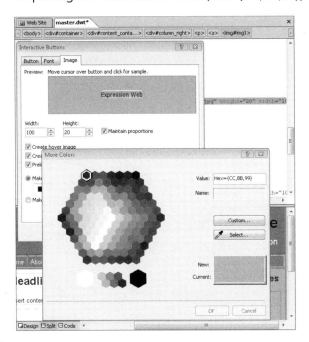

9. Click **OK** in the **More Colors** dialog box, and then click **OK** in the **Interactive
Buttons** dialog box to insert the button on the page

Although you could add more buttons by repeating the preceding steps, we will
use the much faster method of copying the existing button and pasting it to the
page in the Design pane.

10. Right-click the newly created button, and then click **Copy**. Click just after the button, press ⏑ Shift + ⏎ Enter to insert a line break, and then paste the copied button into the page. Click just after this second copy, and then press ⏑ Shift + ⏎ Enter again to create a new line. Paste another copy of the button in this third line.

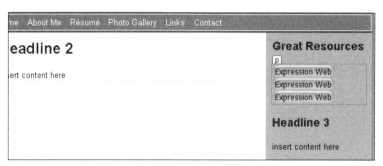

11. In the **Design** pane, double-click the second button to open the **Interactive Buttons** dialog box again, type **CSS Information** in the **Text** box, and then type **http://alistapart.com/** in the **Link** box.

12. Click **OK** to close the dialog box.

13. In the **Design** pane, double-click the third button to open the **Interactive Buttons** dialog box again, type **Web Business** in the **Text** box, and then type **http://sitepoint.com** in the **Link** box. Click **OK** to close the dialog box.

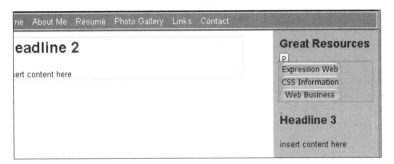

14. Save your page.

The Save Embedded Files dialog box opens.

15. In the **Save Embedded Files** dialog box, click **Change Folder**, click **images**, click **OK**, and then click **OK** in the **Save Embedded Files** dialog box. After Expression Web saves the page and the images, update the pages that are attached to this Dynamic Web Template.

16. Open the *default.htm* page, and then preview it in a browser.

> **Note** If you're using Windows Internet Explorer 7, its default behavior is to block the running of *scripts* and *ActiveX* controls. You will see a yellow warning banner above the page you're previewing. Click the warning, click Allow Blocked Content, and then click Yes in the warning confirmation.

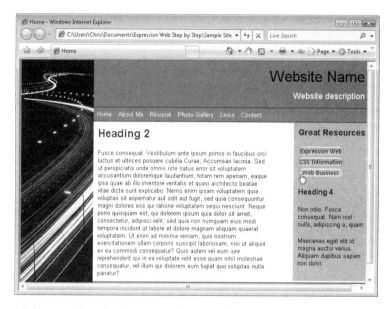

Make sure that the interactive buttons behave as you expected, and browse through the pages of this site template to make sure that the buttons are present on all of the pages. Pay particular attention to the background color of the button and to what happens when the mouse pointer is over the button.

17. Close your browser, and switch to Expression Web.

 BE SURE TO leave the *CH8* site open for use in later exercises.

Using the Interactive Buttons feature is very easy. If you take full advantage of it, you'll have a tremendous number of possible visual combinations, and these buttons are flexible enough to be used convincingly in any page area.

Because this sample site is attached to a Dynamic Web Template, inserting the interactive buttons into all of the pages at once was also a snap. Maintaining all of the buttons on all of the pages—that is, adding, changing, or deleting buttons—can be done by editing one single template file, and the update will cascade to all pages that are attached to it.

Using Layers and Behaviors

Expression Web provides a visual interface for performing complicated *dynamic HTML* (*DHTML*) tasks. These tasks are accomplished by using Expression Web's Layers and Behaviors task panes. In the next exercise, you will examine these capabilities and insert a DHTML-driven "viewer" into one of your pages. This viewer will allow you to show information to a visitor in several ways without requiring navigation to different pages.

In this exercise, you will use the Interactive Buttons feature and the Layers and Behaviors panes to create a multimedia display area in your page.

USE the *CH8* site you modified in the previous exercise.

OPEN the *CH8* site if it isn't already open, and then display the *default.htm* page.

1. In the **Design** pane, delete **Headline 2**, and then type **Dynamic Presentation**. Click the layout text, click **<p>** on the quick tag selector bar, and then press ⌫. On the **Insert** menu, point to **HTML**, and then click **<div>**.

A new DIV element is placed in the page.

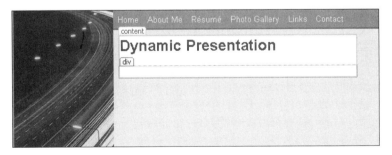

2. Save your page, and then click **<div>** on the quick tag selector bar for the DIV element that you just placed in the page. On the **Apply Styles** task pane, click **New Style**. Change the **Selector** box to **#controls**, select the **Apply new style to document selection** check box, click **Existing style sheet** in the **Define in** list, and then type **styles/style3.css** (the document's current style sheet) in the **URL** box.

3. In the **Category** list, click **Background**. Click the **background-color** arrow, and then click **More Colors**.

4. In the **More Colors** dialog box that opens, click **Select**, use the eyedropper to select the background color of the main navigation bar (*#92856A*), and then click **OK**.

5. In the **Category** list, click **Position**, type **300px** in the **width** box, and then type **270px** in the **height** box. Click **OK** to set your changes and close the dialog box.

6. In the **Design** pane, click this newly styled DIV element. On the **Insert** menu, click **Interactive Button** to show the **Interactive Buttons** dialog box.

7. In the **Interactive Buttons** dialog box, click **Embossed Tab 6** in the **Buttons** list, type **Video** in the **Text** box, and leave the **Link** box empty.

8. Click **OK** to insert the button into the page.

9. Repeat steps 7 and 8 twice more, using **Audio** and **Text Only** for the button **Text** and leaving the **Link** box empty.

A row of three buttons is created, with no spaces between the buttons.

10. On the **Insert** menu, click **HTML,** and then click **<div>**.

A new DIV element is inserted into the page.

11. Click the new DIV element, and then in the **Manage Styles** pane, click **New Style** to open the **New Style** dialog box.

12. Type **#presentation** in the **Selector** box, and select the **Apply new style to document selection** check box. In the **Define in** list, click **Existing style sheet**, and then type **style3.css** in the **URL** box. In the **Category** list, click **Box**, and then type **30px** in the **padding** box below **padding**. In the **Category** list, click **Position**, type **180px** in the **height** box, and then type **240px** in the **width** box. Click **OK** to close the dialog box.

Insert Layer

13. Click inside the new DIV element and then click **Layers** on the **Format** menu. In the **Layers** task pane, click **Insert Layer**.

Expression Web inserts a layer below your row of buttons.

14. In the **Layers** task pane, right-click **layer1**, and then click **Modify ID**. Change the **ID** to **player**. Right-click **player**, and then click **Borders and Shading**. On the **Shading** tab, change the **Background color** to **white**, and then click **OK**. Right-click **player** again, and then click **Positioning**. Type **240px** in the **width** box, type **180px** in the **height** box, and then click **OK**.

15. Click inside this newly styled DIV element, and type **Please select a viewing option by clicking one of the buttons above**. Save your page and click **OK** in the **Save Embedded Files** dialog box.

16. In the **Folder List**, open the *video-code.txt* file from the *media* folder. Select the code, and copy it to the Clipboard. Close the file, and switch to *default.htm*. In the **Design** pane, click the **Video** interactive button, and then click **Behaviors** on the **Format** menu to show the **Behaviors** task pane. In the **Behaviors** task pane, click **Insert**, point to **Set Text**, and then click **Set Text of Layer.**

17. In the **Set Text of Layer** dialog box that opens, paste the code from the Clipboard into the **New HTML** box, and then click **OK** to set your changes.

18. In the **Folder List**, open the *text-code.txt* file from the *media* folder. Select the code, and copy it to the Clipboard. Close the file, and switch to *default.htm*. In the **Design** pane, click the **Text Only** interactive button. On the **Behaviors** task pane, click **Insert**, point to **Set Text**, and then click **Set Text of Layer**. Paste the code from the Clipboard into the **New HTML** box, and then click **OK** to set your changes.

19. In the **Folder List**, open the *audio-code.txt* file from the *media* folder. Select the code, and copy it to the Clipboard. Close the file, and switch to *default.htm*. In the **Design** pane, click the **Audio** interactive button. In the **Behaviors** task pane, click **Insert**, point to **Set Text**, and then click **Set Text of Layer**. Paste the code from the Clipboard into the **New HTML** box, and then click **OK** to set your changes.

20. Save your page and preview it in a browser. Explore your creation in the browser by clicking the buttons to check each delivery method.

 BE SURE TO leave the *CH8* site open for use in later exercises.

Although the video and audio files were provided for this exercise, consider the outcome: using only the user interface in Expression Web, you were able to set up a nice three-button rollover bar, and to set up the capability to deliver content to a visitor in three different ways. Consider also that by using the Set Text Of Layer function, no extra files will be downloaded unless the site visitor clicks one of the buttons. This way, the visitor can receive your page quickly, and can then click for "heavy" content such as video or audio. It's a much better user experience than if the running media content were placed on the surface of the page.

Using Personal Web Packages

If you're an experienced site designer, you've probably amassed a large collection of files and scripts such as shopping carts or database applications that you tend to use in all or most sites that you create. If you're very new to Web design, you will probably begin to develop this type of collection very soon.

In Chapter 2, "Moving from FrontPage to Expression Web," you saw how the Code Snippet Library helps you to save and access snippets of code that you'll use frequently; but it's not the best tool if you're looking for lots of functionality or for working with collections of scripts. The Personal Web Package is the tool you'll want.

With a Personal Web Package, you can export a collection of scripts or other assets from within a site; and you can save all of the data to a single file (an *FWP* file), which you can save on your local computer or distribute by any method you want, such as e-mail or a link on a Web site.

After a collection of files has been exported as an .fwp file, it can be imported very easily by any Expression Web user.

Here's a scenario: the *media* folder in the sample site is a project that you want to save to reuse in another site. You can export the *media* folder as a Personal Web Package.

In this exercise, you will export and import a Personal Web Package.

> **USE** the *CH8* sample site you modified in the previous exercise.
> **OPEN** the *CH8* site if it isn't already open.

1. On the **File** menu, point to **Export**, and then click **Personal Web Package** to open the **Export Web Package** dialog box.

2. The **Export Web Package** dialog box checks for file dependencies when you add a page to the export list. For instance, click **media** in the **Files in Web site** list, and then click **Add**. Expression Web will ask if you would like to include the contents of the folder in your Web package. Click **Yes**.

   Notice that the media folder is copied to the Files In Package list. It is copied because the files within the *media* folder don't depend on any files outside that folder.

3. In the **Files in Web site** list, click **default.htm**, and then click **Add**.

Notice that all of the files in the site are now copied to the Files In Package list. That's because the default page is dependent on almost every file in the site: cascading style sheets files, images, the *master.dwt* file, even the pages that it links to.

4. In the **Files in Package** list, select all of the files and folder, and then click **Remove** to clear your export project. In the **Files in Site** list, click **media**, and then click **Add**.

5. Click **Properties** to open the **Web Package Properties** dialog box. Change the name from **My Web Package** to **Media Files**. Add a description, author, and company name if you want.

This information will be contained within the package. In the bottom of the dialog box, you can see a list of external dependencies, which are references to files outside the current site, such as pages that hyperlinks point to or absolute references to images or other files.

6. Click **OK** to close the dialog box.

7. In the **Export Web Package** dialog box, click **OK**.

The **File Save** dialog box opens.

8. In the **File Save** dialog box, navigate to a location where you want to save the exported Web package, and then click **Save**.

Web package exports can really bolster your long-term asset and workflow building. Imagine setting up your favorite shopping cart, a package of utility-type scripts you use, and a few other items in logical arrangements as Web packages. You'd be able to easily bring them into any project that is open in Expression Web with only a few clicks.

> **Note** You can use Web Package exports to cull files. If you've been working on a project for a while, the site probably has become loaded with revisions, old files, and all the other artifacts that a project tends to produce. If you want to pare the project down to the essential pieces—for instance, to send it to a customer or as a preparatory step before publishing to a server—you could select only the files you need and let Expression Web take care of adding the dependent files to your export list.
>
> You can simply export the Web Package and send it off to someone else, or you can create an empty site and import it. Regardless of how you use the Web Package, it's a fast way to isolate only the files you need and leave unnecessary files behind.

9. On the **File** menu, point to **Import**, and then click **Personal Web Package** to open the **File Open** dialog box. Navigate to the *Documents\Microsoft Press\Expression Web SBS\Sample Files* folder, click the *CH8.fwp* file, and then click **Open**.

The Import Web Package dialog box opens. In this dialog box, you can select or deselect files and folders and view the properties of the Web package.

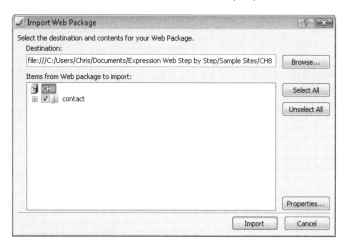

10. Click **Import** to import the *contact* folder and the files it contains to the root of your site.

11. In the security warning dialog box that opens, click **Run** to continue the process of importing the contents of this Web package.

12. Click **OK** in the deployment complete message box to complete the process.

A file named *confirmation.aspx* now exists in your site *contact* folder. This folder and its contents will be used in the next exercise, in which you will work with forms.

 BE SURE TO leave the *CH8* site open for use in later exercises.

Personal Web Packages make certain functionality, graphics, and other assets portable. In addition to the portability benefit, the export process can be helpful in enabling you to package only files you want to keep and to discard unnecessary files.

Creating and Using Forms

Forms are a feature that enables you to provide varied levels of user interaction. Forms can be used for anything from the most complex database application to the simplest of e-mail-producing **contact forms**. Expression Web provides several tools to assist in the creation of forms. All of the tools are available in the Toolbox pane, under the Form Control group.

In this exercise, you will create a simple contact form and configure it to handle the user input.

USE the *CH8* sample site you modified in the previous exercise.
OPEN the *CH8* site if it isn't already open, and then display the *contact.htm* page.

1. In the **Design** pane, click after the last numbered item under the heading **Driving Directions**, and then press ⏎ Enter twice to break out of the ordered list and create a new paragraph.

2. Type **Contact Form**, and press [Enter] again to start a new paragraph. Select the text you just typed, click the **Style** arrow on the toolbar, and then click **Heading 3 <h3>**.

3. Click in the paragraph below the H3 element. If the **Toolbox** task pane isn't visible, on the **Task Panes** menu, click **Toolbox**. In the **Toolbox** task pane, expand **Form Controls**.

These form controls can be added to your page either by dragging them from the toolbox to where you want them or by setting the cursor in the design surface of the page where you want them and double-clicking their entry in the toolbox. You might also find it helpful to use Split view.

4. In the **Design** pane, click the P element below the heading you entered. On the quick tag selector bar, click **<p>** to select the entire element, and then double-click **Form** in the **Toolbox** pane.

An empty form is inserted into your page in place of the paragraph.

5. Type **Name**, and then press [Shift] + [Enter] to insert a line break. In the **Toolbox** task pane, double-click **Input (Text)** to insert a text field.

6. Right-click the text field, and then click **Form Field Properties** to open the **Text Box Properties** dialog box. Type **name** in the **Name** box, type **1** in the **Tab order** box, and then click **OK** to set the changes and close the dialog box.

7. Click just after the text field, and then press ⌈Shift⌉＋⌈Enter⌉ to insert a line break.

8. Type **E-mail** and then press ⌈Shift⌉＋⌈Enter⌉ to insert a line break. In the **Toolbox** task pane, double-click **Input (Text)** to insert another text field.

9. Right-click the new text field, and then click **Form Field Properties**. Type **email** in the **Name** box, type **2** in the **Tab order** box, and then click **OK** to set the changes and close the dialog box. Click just after the text field, and then press ⌈Shift⌉＋⌈Enter⌉ to insert a line break.

10. Type **Phone**, and then press ⌈Shift⌉＋⌈Enter⌉ to insert a line break. In the **Toolbox** task pane, double-click **Input (Text)** to insert another text field.

11. Right-click the new text field, and then click **Form Field Properties**. Type **phone** in the **Name** box, type **3** in the **Tab order** box, and then click **OK** to set the changes and close the dialog box. Click just after the text field, and then press ⌈Shift⌉＋⌈Enter⌉ to insert a line break.

12. Type **Your Message**, and then press ⌈Shift⌉＋⌈Enter⌉ to insert a new line break. In the **Toolbox** task pane, double-click **Text Area** to insert a text area field into your form.

13. Right-click the text area field, and then click **Form Field Properties** to open the **TextArea Box Properties** dialog box. Type **message** in the **Name** box, type **40** in the **Width in characters** box, type **4** in the **Tab order** box, type **10** in the **Number of lines** box, and then click **OK** to set the changes and close the dialog box.

14. Click just after the text area field, and then press ⌈Shift⌋+⌈Enter⌋ to insert a line break. In the **Toolbox** task pane, double-click **Input (Reset)**, and then double-click **Input (Submit)**.

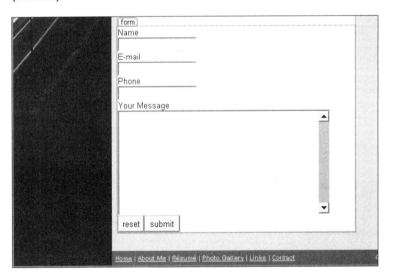

After setting the form field names and tab order, you can configure what happens when a site visitor uses the form by filling in the requested information and clicking the Submit button.

15. In the **Design** pane, right-click anywhere inside the form, and then click **Form Properties** to open the **Form Properties** dialog box.

> **Note** There are options on the Form Properties dialog box for features that require Microsoft Office FrontPage server extensions. These options require not only FrontPage server extensions but also require that e-mail transport be enabled in some cases and require FrontPage publishing. FTP publishing will cause them to fail. These FrontPage options are present only to enable an Expression Web user to edit pages that were originally created in FrontPage and that use FrontPage extensions.

The Send To Other option is selected.

16. Type **Contact** in the **Form name** box, and then click **Options**. In the **Action** box of the **Options for Custom Form Handler** dialog box, type **confirmation.aspx**, and then click **OK** to set your changes.

17. Click **OK** in the **Form Properties** dialog box, and then save the page.

18. Open the *confirmation.aspx* file from the *contact* folder. On the **Format** menu, point to **Dynamic Web Template**, and then click **Update Selected Page**.

> **Note** If *confirmation.aspx* isn't in the *contact* folder you must import the file. See step 9 of the exercise in "Using Personal Web Packages," earlier in this chapter.

19. Save and preview *confirmation.aspx* in a browser. In the browser, click the **Contact** link, fill out the form, and then click **submit**.

The confirmation page shows the form input.

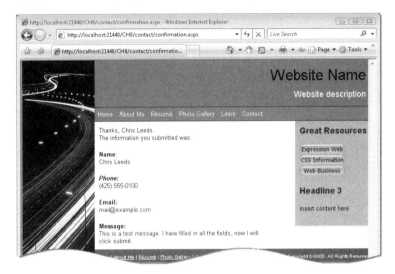

> **Note** The confirmation page is only intended to illustrate how to configure an HTML form in Expression Web. It is assumed that the site developer will have a script or form handler to submit an HTML form to.

 CLOSE the *CH8* site and any open Internet Explorer windows. If you are not continuing directly to the next chapter, exit Expression Web.

Key Points

- The Interactive Buttons feature provides a quick and easy way to provide attractive roll-over buttons without the need to use an image editor or write code to animate the buttons.

- You can use functionality from the Layers and Behaviors task panes to create interesting visual features and provide for user interaction without the need to write JavaScript code.

- Personal Web Packages provide a useful method for exporting files from or importing files to an Expression Web site.

- Expression Web provides tools to build and configure the actions of forms. Expression Web's Form Properties dialog box is also compatible with forms that were built by using FrontPage.

Chapter at a Glance

Publish by using
FTP or HTTP,
pages 206 and 212

Publish to a
disk location,
page 218

9 Publishing a Web Site

In this chapter, you will learn to:

✔ Consider hosting requirements.

✔ Find and register a domain name.

✔ Use Microsoft Office Live.

✔ Publish by using FTP.

✔ Publish by using HTTP.

✔ Publish to a disk location.

After you've taken all the time and trouble to create a Web site and get everything set up the way you want, you are probably going to want people to be able to access it. Whether it's a site for only a select group of users (an *intranet site*), or a site for the general public (an *Internet site*), you will need the files and folders in your *local site* to reside on a *server*.

From a Microsoft Expression Web standpoint, moving the local files and folders that comprise your site to a server is where *publishing* comes in. Although publishing might, on its surface, seem like simply copying files from your local site to a server, there's actually a lot more going on during this operation. In addition to the publishing operation to copy the files and folders from one place to another, Expression Web will also keep tabs on what's been published, where it's been published to, and when each file was last published. Add to that the fact that, with Expression Web, you can publish not only from your local site to a server but also from a server back down to your local computer, or even from one server to another server without involving your local computer at all, and the complexity and usefulness of the publishing functions of Expression Web become quite apparent.

From within Expression Web, you have four choices for publishing:

- Microsoft Office FrontPage Server Extensions publishing

    - Requires FrontPage Server Extensions on the server

    - Provides for encrypted transfer of user name and passwords by publishing by using the *HTTP* protocol

    - Allows for maximum exploitation of Expression Web's features and greater security than *FTP* publishing

- *WebDAV* publishing

    - Requires Distributed Authoring and Versioning (DAV) to be set up on the server

    - Is currently fairly rare but provides a feature set that is otherwise not available

    See Also For more information, visit *www.webdav.org*.

- FTP publishing

    - Requires File Transfer Protocol (FTP) to be set up on the server

    - Is the most common and widely available form of publishing

- File System publishing

    - Publishes a *disk-based site* from one folder structure to another

    - Is generally used to "copy" a site from one location on your computer to another for administrative purposes

    - Has no requirements, but also results in minimal capabilities at the publish location

In this chapter, you'll be introduced to the various types of publishing and to the publishing prerequisites, such as securing a domain name and *hosting* for your site.

> **Important** Before you can use the practice files in this chapter, you need to install them from the book's companion CD to their default location. See "Using the Book's CD" on page xiii for more information.

> **Troubleshooting** Graphics and operating system–related instructions in this book reflect the Windows Vista user interface. If your computer is running Windows XP and you experience trouble following the instructions as written, please refer to the "Information for Readers Running Windows XP" section at the beginning of this book.

Considering Hosting Requirements

There are many server types on which you can host your domain and site. For the purposes of this discussion, we will divide them into two main categories: those that run a Microsoft Windows operating system, and those that do not run a Windows operating system.

The decision about which server type to use depends solely on what kind of files and functionality you either have currently in your site or plan to include in the future. Use these guidelines:

- If your site has or will have Microsoft dynamic pages such as *ASP.NET*, or ASP files, or if the site requires a *Microsoft Office Access* or *Microsoft SQL Server database*, you should choose a Windows server with the appropriate Microsoft .NET Framework version or the appropriate *database* capabilities.

- If your site has or will have non-Windows dynamic pages such as PHP or a *MySQL* server, then you could use a non-Windows server, although PHP and MySQL run fine on a Windows server if the server administrator configures and allows it.

- If your site has only static pages (.htm/.html) and you don't intend to add server-side functionality, it really doesn't matter which server type you choose.

When choosing a server to host your site, it's important to make a good decision right away. It can be a tremendous hassle to move a site after it's been deployed to a server. The decision is complicated by the fact that there are literally tens of thousands of hosts you can choose from. A little due diligence is definitely required on this topic. A good place to start, by using the experience of others, is at *www.webhostingtalk.com*.

Some of the things you'll need after signing up for hosting space include:

- User name and password for publishing. Whether you opt for HTTP, FTP, or WebDAV, you will be issued a unique user name and password.

- The URL or folder you are supposed to publish into. Some hosts have a specific folder in your Web space that you must publish into.

- The *DNS* settings your host requires you to use. To enable visitors to arrive at your site on your hosting space, you will need to use the appropriate DNS settings. These settings are changed within the account where you registered your domain name. At least two DNS entries are required—for example, *NS1.EXAMPLE.COM* and *NS2.EXAMPLE.COM*. When you change these settings at your *registrar*, it can take up to 72 hours for the settings to propagate throughout the Internet.

After you set up your hosting space, you'll be ready to move on to publishing your files and folders to the Internet. Resist the urge to find the cheapest host, or to make a quick decision. This is one of those points where taking some additional time in the beginning can save you much more time and trouble in the future.

> **Reseller Accounts**
>
> If you're a professional Web designer, or if you intend to get into the business, you should look into what's commonly known as a *reseller account*. Such an account will allow you to host your own site and all your customers' sites. You'll be able to access all the sites through a common control panel, and your clients will be able to access their own domain settings through their own unique *domain control panel*.
>
> One provider of reseller accounts is High End Host (*www.highendhost.com*). Because a reseller account hosts not only your site but also your customers' sites that you're responsible for, even more weight must be placed on due diligence in the beginning. Reselling hosting to your customers can be very easy and profitable if you have the right host, or it can be a recipe for disaster if you have the wrong host. You can check *www.webhostingtalk.com* for reseller accounts also.

Finding and Registering a Domain Name

In addition to having hosting space for your site, you'll also need a ***domain name***. A domain name is the base of the alphanumeric address called the **URL** (Uniform Resource Locator), and it's the address visitors use to find a site. For example, Microsoft's URL is *www.microsoft.com*, and their domain name is *microsoft.com*.

When you register your domain name, you will want to use your name, your company's name, or a word or phrase that's directly related to the products or services your company provides. It's important to give a great deal of thought to the domain name you choose, because it will have direct impact on search engine relevance of all the pages within your site. In addition, it's the name you'll tell people, and whether you tell them in print advertising, by phone, or in person, the name needs to be descriptive and easy to remember and spell.

> **Tip** Even if you need only one site, that doesn't necessarily mean you should have only one domain. You might want to register your company name with several extensions, such as *example.com*, *example.net*, and *example.org*. Another tactic is to register common misspellings of your "main" domain. That way, if visitors happen to type the domain name improperly, you can still deliver them to the site.

Part of the choice in registering a domain name is the extension. Common *domain extensions* are: .com (intended for company and commercial sites), .net (intended for network sites), .org (intended for organizations), and .edu (intended for educational institutions). There are a great number of new domain extensions available today, but you should initially use the one that was designed for your site's purpose and profile.

For domain names to function as intended, it's absolutely necessary that each name be unique. Therefore, each domain name is registered. Registration of names is overseen by the Internet Corporation for Assigned Names and Numbers (*ICANN*).

Because there are a tremendous number of registrars where you can set up and regis-ter your domain name, you should do some research. ICANN's site, at *www.internic.com*, maintains a list of accredited registrars along with invaluable information on the topic. There's a lot of information, so this is another situation where learning from other people's experience will pay off exponentially. Expect to pay between $7 and $30 per year for a registered domain.

> **Note** People who are in business as Web site designers or developers might want to look into reselling domain name registration as well as reselling accounts for hosting. You will make less money than you will with reselling hosting space, but the added level of convenience of having all your customers' domains registered through a com-mon domain control panel might be worth it for you. Two of the most popular options are *www.wildwestdomains.com* and *www.enom.com*, though they each have different methodologies. A number of domain name reselling options are available, so this, as with all major decisions, also requires some research.

Using Microsoft Office Live

One possible solution for registering a domain name and setting up hosting in one step would be Microsoft's new option: Office Live. Three levels of service are available at *www.officelive.com*, which range from a free domain registration and Web site to a $39.95 per month plan that offers enhanced space, bandwidth, and the ability to use editors such as Expression Web, Microsoft Office FrontPage, and third-party editors. Only the free plan (Office Live Basics) disallows using third-party editors; but all of the plans offer some form of free trial usage. Office Live might be just what you're looking for, so you should spend some time checking it out.

> **Note** In my research for this book, I found the Office Live servers to be the absolute fast-est servers I'd ever published to. I found it convenient that the user name and password were the same as the Windows Live ID that I used when I signed up for them.

Publishing by Using FTP

Publishing by using FTP is a valuable capability, because virtually every server and every hosting space has FTP publishing available. It's definitely the most common method of transferring files to a server. Even if you prefer to use HTTP publishing, as many people do, a time will come when you need to use FTP. For example, you have a new customer with an existing Web site and you need to copy his online assets down to your local computer. If FrontPage Server Extensions do not exist on his hosting space, you won't have a choice, and you'll need to use FTP to transfer the files and folders from his Web space down to your computer. Knowing when and how to use FTP is a valuable skill, and it's one you will undoubtedly need sometime.

In this exercise, you will publish a site to a server by using FTP, and you'll become familiar with the publishing settings that are available in Expression Web for FTP publishing.

USE the *CH9* sample site. This site is located in the *Documents\Microsoft Press\Expression Web SBS\Sample Sites* folder.

BE SURE TO start Expression Web and have your FTP user name and password available, before beginning this exercise.

OPEN the *CH9* site.

1. On the **File** menu, click **Publish Site.**

   The Remote Web Site Properties dialog box opens, displaying the most recent publishing destination and method used.

2. Click **FTP.** In the **Remote Web site location** box, type the FTP address of the location you will publish the site to.

   You should have received this information from your host.

3. In the **FTP directory** box, type the name of the folder that your public files will reside in. Your host may or may not require you to use a specific folder for your public files. If they don't require one, leave this field blank.

   Note In the exercises in this chapter, you will see references in the graphics to *ExpressionWebStepbyStep.com.* This domain was set up specifically for the publishing operations demonstrated in this book.

4. Click **OK**.

Expression Web prompts you for your FTP site user name and password.

> **Note** When you try to publish by using FTP, you will see a warning in the logon dialog box that states: "FTP transmits the user name and password without encryption. If possible, open the Web site by using an HTTP URL to help protect it from potential network attacks." This is one good reason to have your host apply FrontPage Server Extensions to your Web site's account so that you can publish by using HTTP.

5. Enter your credentials in the logon dialog box, and click **OK**.

Expression Web displays the local and remote sites in Remote Web Site view.

> **Note** When you log on to your site for the first time, you might see some folders in your site structure. This is generally normal; these folders are put there by your host. Often they're for *server logs*, Control Panel files, and so on.

6. At the top of the **Remote Web Site** view, click **Remote Web Site Properties**.

The Remote Web Site Properties dialog box opens.

7. You've already used the initial **Remote Web Site** tab, so click the **Optimize HTML** tab.

8. To enable the HTML optimization options, select the **When publishing, optimize HTML by removing the following elements** check box.

> **Important** These options are self-explanatory. In many cases, Expression Web will rely on these comments and attributes being in the page code and that's why they're only removed when they're published to the server. One thing to keep in mind regarding using these optimization features is that if you strip out *comments* and attributes that Expression Web needs and then publish from the server to your local computer, you will experience some usability issues when you edit the site in Expression Web.

9. Click the **Publishing** tab in the **Remote Web Site Properties** dialog box.

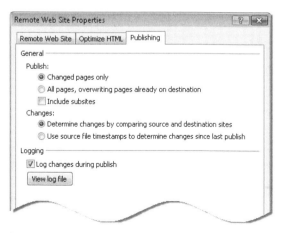

> **Note** The options on this tab are also self-explanatory. You might change them from their defaults for issues relating to publishing speed or a publishing strategy. For example, if the application takes too long and **times out** while it is comparing files on the server to files in the local site, you can select the option to use **time stamps** rather than comparison. If your local site contains **subsites**, you might choose the option to publish subsites on certain occasions. In general, the Publish tab default settings don't require change.

Take some time to familiarize yourself with the options on this tab. Another useful option enables you to choose whether you want the publishing operations to be logged and provides a link to view the *log file*.

10. Click **OK** to close the dialog box.

11. At the bottom of the **Remote Web Site** view, click **Publish Web site**.

During the publishing operation, the Status area in the lower-left corner of the workspace displays messages regarding the files being published.

> **Important** When using the Changed Pages Only option for publishing, if Expression Web finds files or folders on the server that aren't present in the local site, you will be asked if you want to remove them. If you aren't absolutely sure you want the files or folders removed, click No.

12. If your site uses metadata, a warning dialog box will appear. Because you're not using any FrontPage features and are purposely publishing by using FTP, click **OK**.

Publishing finishes and the Remote Web Site view shows a status message that indicates this status. There are also links below the status message to view the publish log file or open the remote Web site in Expression Web.

You have now published a local site to a remote server by using FTP in Expression Web. All of your local files are now on the server, and you can view them in a browser. Simply open a browser and type your site's domain in the address bar to check your work.

CLOSE any open Internet Explorer windows.

BE SURE TO leave the *CH9* site open for use in the next exercise.

> **Troubleshooting** Sometimes the hosting service places a *default file* in the root folder of your account. *Index.htm, index.html, default.htm,* and *default.html* are common default files for a Web server. If you publish your site and upon visiting the domain in a browser you don't see the home page that you published, you will need to delete or rename the default file that the host created. Then your site's home page will take precedence and be passed to the browser as the default file of the domain. You can perform this action in Expression Web in the Remote Web Site view by right-clicking the index file your hosting company supplied in the Remote Web Site pane and clicking either Delete or Rename.

> **Important** If you intend to publish your Expression Web site by using FTP, it's recommended that you use the built-in FTP publishing rather than a *third-party FTP client*. The reason for this is that Expression Web won't publish the *hidden folders* containing the site's metadata, but a third-party application won't make the distinction and will publish everything. This can often result in a longer than necessary publishing time and a larger than necessary cumulative folder size on the server.

Publishing by Using HTTP

The most solid and secure publishing method from within Expression Web is HTTP publishing. Although FrontPage Server Extensions are required on the *hosting account*, you don't need to rely on FrontPage features. The HTTP method provides the added benefit of *encoding* the user name and password that you use when publishing and can allow for publishing through a *Secure Sockets Layer* (SSL/HTTPS) if you have a *Secure Server Certificate* installed on your server space.

In this exercise, you will use HTTP publishing through Expression Web, and you will use the features that are available with this method.

> **USE** the *CH9* sample site. This site is located in the *Documents\Microsoft Press\Expression Web SBS\Sample Sites* folder.
> **OPEN** the *CH9* site if it is not already open.

1. On the **File** menu, click **Publish Site.**

The Remote Web Site Properties dialog box opens, displaying the most recent publishing destination and method used.

> **Troubleshooting** If a server logon dialog box opens, click Cancel.

2. Click **FrontPage Server Extensions**. In the **Remote Web site location** box, type the HTTP address you will publish to.

> **Note** In the exercises in this chapter, you will see references in the graphics to *ExpressionWebStepbyStep.com*. This domain was set up specifically for the publishing operations demonstrated in this book.

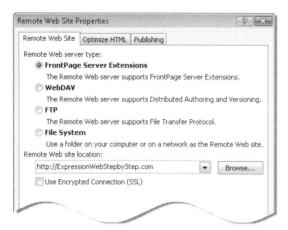

3. Click **OK**. You will be prompted for your FrontPage user name and password.

4. Type your credentials into the logon dialog box, and click **OK**. If you want Expression Web to remember your user name and password, be sure to select the **Remember my password** check box.

The logon dialog box closes, and Expression Web switches to Remote Web Site view.

> **Note** When you log on to your site for the first time you may see some folders in your site structure. This is generally normal and these folders are put there by your host. Often they're for *server logs*, Control Panel files, and so on.

5. At the top of the **Remote Web Site** view, click **Remote Web Site Properties**.

The Remote Web Site Properties dialog box opens.

6. You've already used the initial **Remote Web Site** tab, so click the **Optimize HTML** tab.

7. To enable the HTML optimization options, click the **When publishing, optimize HTML by removing the following elements** check box.

> **Important** These options are self-explanatory. In many cases Expression Web will rely on these comments and attributes being in the page code and that's why they're only removed when they're published to the server. One thing to keep in mind regarding using these optimization features is that if you strip out comments and attributes Expression Web needs and then publish from the server to your local system, you will experience some usability issues when you edit the site in Expression Web.

8. In the **Remote Web Site Properties** dialog box, click the **Publishing** tab.

> **Note** The options on this tab are also self-explanatory. Generally a user will change them from their defaults for issues relating to publishing speed or a *publishing strategy*.
>
> For example, if the application takes too long and times out comparing files on the server to files in the local site, a user can select the option to use time stamps rather than comparison. If the user's local site contains subsites, he or she might on certain occasions choose the option to publish subsites. The Publish tab default settings are usually appropriate.

9. Take some time to familiarize yourself with the options on this tab.

Another useful option enables you to choose whether you want the publishing operations to be logged and provides a link to view the log file.

10. Click **OK** to close the dialog box.

11. At the bottom of the **Remote Web Site** view, click **Publish Web site**.

During the publishing operation, the Status area in the lower-left corner of the workspace displays messages regarding the files being published.

> **Note** When using the Changed Pages Only option for publishing, if Expression Web finds files or folders on the server that aren't present in the local site, you will be asked if you want to remove them. If you aren't absolutely sure you want the files or folders removed, click No.

Publishing finishes, and your Remote Web Site view shows a status message that indicates this status. There are also links below the status message to view the publish log file, view the remote Web site, or open the remote Web site in Expression Web.

12. Click **View your Remote Web site** beneath the status message to open your site in a browser.

You have now published a local site to a remote server by using HTTP in Expression Web. All of your local files are now on the server, and you have viewed them in a browser.

CLOSE any open Internet Explorer windows.

BE SURE TO leave the *CH9* site open for use in the next exercise.

Publishing to a Disk Location

File system or disk location publishing is generally used to "copy" a site from one location on your computer or *local network* to another. You might find yourself needing to use this method in order to move a site from a folder location where you work on sites to another folder location where you archive finished work; or you might want to move a site from its existing folder location to a *network share* on your local network so that you can view it through a browser.

The method of publishing from disk location to disk location is superior to copying in Windows Explorer, because publishing will ensure that all of your files that are necessary are moved and that none of the unnecessary ones are moved. It's the best way to move a site and not run into problems with the metadata that Expression Web uses to manage sites.

USE the *CH9* sample site. This site is located in the *Documents\Microsoft Press\Expression Web SBS\Sample Sites* folder.

OPEN the *CH9* site if it is not already open.

1. On the **File** menu, click **Publish Site.**

   The Remote Web Site Properties dialog box opens.

   > **Troubleshooting** This dialog box will remember the last publish destination and method you used. If you receive a server log on dialog box, click Cancel.

2. Click **File System**, click **Browse**, and then navigate to the local folder in which you want to publish the site.

   > **Note** You can create a local folder location in the New Publish Location dialog box, or you can browse to *Documents\Microsoft Press\Expression Web SBS\Sample Sites\CH9*.

3. Create or select the folder you want, and then click **Open**.

4. In the **Remote Web Site Properties** dialog box, click **OK**.

Expression Web switches to Remote Web Site view.

5. At the top of the **Remote Web Site** view, click **Remote Web Site Properties**. Then in the **Remote Web Site Properties** dialog box, click the **Optimize HTML** tab.

6. To enable the HTML optimization options, select the **When publishing, optimize HTML by removing the following elements** check box.

> **Important** These options are self-explanatory. In many cases Expression Web will rely on these comments and attributes being in the page code, and that's why they're only removed when they're published to the server. If you strip out comments and attributes that Expression Web needs and then publish from the remote site to your local system, you will experience some usability issues when you edit the site in Expression Web.

7. In the **Remote Web Site Properties** dialog box, click the **Publishing tab**.

> **Note** The options on this tab are also self-explanatory. Generally a user will change them from their defaults for issues relating to publishing speed or a publishing strategy.
>
> For example, if the application takes too long and times out comparing files on the server to files in the local Web, a user can select the option to use time stamps rather than comparison. This will never be an issue in File System publishing. If the user's local site contains subsites, he or she may choose the option to publish subsites on certain occasions. In general, the Publish tab default settings don't require change.

8. Take some time to familiarize yourself with the options on this tab.

Another useful option that you can use is to choose whether you want the publishing operations to be logged and provides a link to view the log file.

9. Click **OK** to close the dialog box.

10. At the bottom of the **Remote Web Site** view, click **Publish Web site**.

During the publishing operation, the Status area in the lower-left corner of the workspace displays messages regarding the files being published.

Because the publishing operation is from one local folder to another local folder, you will find this operation to be the fastest publishing method.

> **Note** If you attempt to publish a local site to another local folder as this exercise does and the local site contains dynamic pages such as classic ASP or ASP.NET, you will be warned. The warning only alerts you to the fact that the dynamic pages won't function as they would on a server. There aren't any such pages in this sample site, but you should be aware of the possibility.

> **Note** When using the Changed Pages Only option for publishing, if Expression Web finds files or folders on the server that aren't present in the local site, you will be asked if you want to remove them. If you aren't absolutely sure you want the files or folders removed, click No.

Publishing finishes, and your Remote Web Site view shows a status message that indicates this status. There are also links below the status message to view the publish log file, view the remote Web site, or open the remote Web site in Expression Web.

11. Click **View your publish log file** beneath the status message.

   Your publish log opens in a browser. This log has an option box that enables you to filter the results for certain operations and makes deducing certain information easier.

> **Tip** Because this publish log file appears in a browser window, you have all the common browser file operations available, such as save and print. This functionality can be helpful if you need to save a record of publishing operations for a customer or to send information to the server administrator to report a problem.

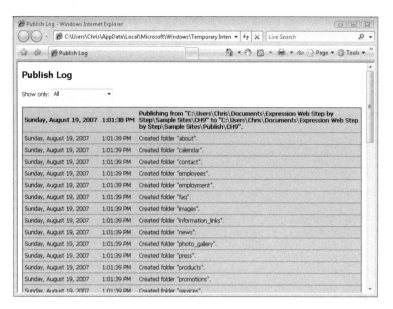

You have now published a local site to a file system location by using Expression Web. All of your local files were moved to a secondary local folder, and you have viewed the publish log file.

 CLOSE the *CH9* site and any open Internet Explorer windows. If you are not continuing directly to the next chapter, exit Expression Web.

Key Points

- Expression Web provides four separate publishing methods: FTP, HTTP (FrontPage Server Extensions), WebDAV, and File System. Each serves a different purpose.

- Although FTP publishing is the most common publishing method, HTTP publishing provides several improved features and more functionality.

- Publishing by using File System is the most accurate and least error prone way to copy a site from one folder location to another.

- You can use WebDAV publishing in Expression Web if you have it set up on your server.

- You can set various publishing options through the Remote Web Site Properties dialog box.

- You can optimize the HTML code of your pages by removing HIML comments, Interactive Button attributes, script comments, and other elements.

Chapter at a Glance

Edit a server-based site, **page 232**

Publish selectively, **page 242**

Use subsites, **page 246**

10 Managing a Web Site

In this chapter, you will learn to:

- ✔ Back up server-based sites.
- ✔ Edit a server-based site.
- ✔ Use site settings.
- ✔ Publish selectively.
- ✔ Use subsites.

Whether you're the owner of a single site or a professional webmaster who is responsible for a great number of sites, one of the requirements you will have is site management. This task takes many forms and comes into play in many parts of the process.

In addition to being a good editing and publishing tool, Microsoft Expression Web contains a number of features that offer the user a management system that's truly second to none. Possibly the most useful of these features is the ability to open and manipulate a site "live" on the server.

In this chapter, you will learn to back up and edit server-based sites, use site settings, publish pages selectively, and use sub sites.

Important Before you can use the practice files in this chapter, you need to install them from the book's companion CD to their default location. See "Using the Book's CD" on page xiii for more information.

Troubleshooting Graphics and operating system–related instructions in this book reflect the Windows Vista user interface. If your computer is running Windows XP and you experience trouble following the instructions as written, please refer to the "Information for Readers Running Windows XP" section at the beginning of this book.

Backing Up Server-Based Sites

Occasionally, the files on a *server-based site* can actually be newer than the files in the local copy of the same site. For example, if the server-based site contains *form data*, is a *shopping cart*, or is a type of *dynamic site* that takes user input, the server-based site will have more or newer information than the local copy. In this case, a backup copy of the server-based site is essential.

Another reason to back up a server-based site is that the local copy might become lost or corrupt, or be compromised in some way. Still another reason to back up a server-based site is that you might acquire a new customer and need all of their online assets to be brought down to your local computer so that you can work on them.

In all of these scenarios and others, Expression Web takes care of everything. To fully exploit its capabilities, all you need is an understanding of how the features function.

In this exercise, you will back up to your local computer a site that exists on a server. No practice files are required for this exercise.

USE your own published site and server parameters for this exercise.

BE SURE TO start Expression Web and have an active Internet connection before beginning this exercise.

1. On the **File** menu, click **Open Site** to show the **Open Site** dialog box.

2. In the **Open Site** dialog box, type the HTTP address of your server into the **Site name** box , and then click **Open**.

This step assumes that your site has FrontPage Server Extensions applied. If it does not, skip to step 8 to follow the FTP method for backing up a server-based site to your local computer.

3. Type your user name and password in the server logon dialog box.

Your server-based site opens in Expression Web.

> **Note** For this exercise, the server-based site that appears in the graphics is the one that was published in Chapter 9, "Publishing a Web Site."

4. On the **File** menu, click **Publish Site**.

The Remote Web Site Properties dialog box opens.

5. Click **File System**, browse to the local folder where you want this backup to reside, and then click **OK**.

> **Note** If you want to create a new location, click New Folder at the top of the New Publish Location dialog box, name the folder, and then click Open.

Expression Web switches to Remote Site view, with the local and remote sites in the workspace.

6. Click **Publish Site**.

Expression Web publishes the site. The status message in the lower-left corner indicates where the publishing operation is in the process and when it finishes.

7. Click **Close Site** on the **File** menu. Expression Web switches to an empty user interface, with no site open.

8. On the **File** menu, click **Open Site**, type the FTP location of your server-based site into the **Site name** box, and then click **Open**.

The Remote Web Site Editing Options dialog box opens. This dialog box enables you to open and edit an FTP site live on the server, or to edit a local copy and publish it at a later time.

9. In the **Remote Web Site Editing Options** dialog box, click **Edit local copy now, and publish changes to the server later**, and then click **OK**.

The function of this option is identical to performing a backup by publishing a server-based site to a local computer.

10. The server logon dialog box opens. Log on with your FTP credentials.

The Web Site Setup dialog box opens.

11. Type the site's root directory into the **Root Directory** box.

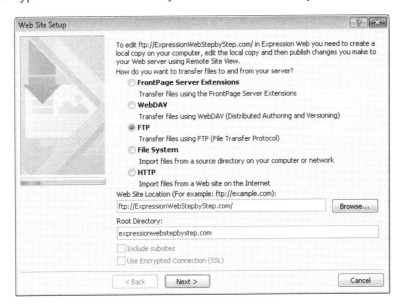

12. Click **Next** to start the **Import Web Site Wizard**. On the wizard's first page, click **Browse**.

The New Publish Location dialog box opens.

13. Browse to a location on your local computer to which you want to copy the site. Either click an existing folder, or create a new one by clicking the **New Folder** button at the top of the dialog box. After selecting the appropriate location, click **Open**.

You are returned to the Import Web Site Wizard, with the name of the folder that you clicked in the previous step now in the Local Copy Location box.

14. Click **Next**. Then on the final page of the wizard, click **Finish**.

The wizard closes, and Expression Web switches to Remote Web Site view.

15. Click **Publish Web site**.

Publishing from the FTP site to the file system location begins. As publishing continues, the status message indicates where the publishing operation is in the process.

Publishing finishes when activity in the status message at the bottom of the workspace stops and the Publish Web Site button becomes active again.

 CLOSE your site and any open Internet Explorer windows.

You've just published a server-based site to your local computer to create a backup. Expression Web enables you to publish such a site by using either the HTTP or the FTP method.

The more frequently you back up a site, the more secured the data will be. These backup methods are also necessary for working on a site that has never been stored on your local computer, such as when you need a copy of a new customer's site to work on, or when you need a copy of a site for archival purposes.

> **Note** One little-known feature of HTTP publishing is that you can open the server-based site and publish it to another server-based location. This feature can be useful in a number of situations; your local computer and local Internet connection are bypassed, and local connection speed is negated.

Editing Server-Based Sites

Occasionally, you will want to make a change directly to a server-based site. Rather than changing a local file and publishing it, you can make the changes directly to the files that reside on the server.

One reason for editing directly on the server is that you might not have access to a computer that contains a local copy of the site.

Another common reason to work on a server-based site is that you might be trying to fine-tune some server-side scripting and want to bypass the process of changing a local file, publishing it, and then checking the server-based file with a browser. By working directly on the server, you can make your change and test it, all from within the Expression Web user interface.

In this exercise, you will make changes directly to a server-based site. No practice files are required.

> **USE** your own published site and server parameters for this exercise.
> **BE SURE TO** have an active Internet connection before beginning this exercise.

1. On the **File** menu, click **Open Site.** In the **Open Site** dialog box, type the HTTP address of the server-based site you want to open, and then click **Open**.

> **Troubleshooting** This step assumes that your site has FrontPage Server Extensions applied. If it does not, skip to step 10 to follow the FTP method for editing a site directly on the server.

The server logon dialog box opens.

2. Type your user name and password in this dialog box, and then click **OK**.

The server-based site opens in Expression Web.

3. Open any page in the site and make a change. It doesn't matter what you change, as long as you can recognize it when you view the file in a browser. Then click **Save**.

4. Click **Preview**.

The server-based Web page opens in a browser, and the change that you made is visible.

5. Close your browser, and switch to Expression Web.

6. On the **File** menu, point to **New**, and then click **Create From Dynamic Web Template**.

The Attach Dynamic Web Template dialog box opens.

7. Click **master.dwt**, and then click **Open**.

Expression Web creates a new page based on the selected Dynamic Web Template.

8. Click **Save**. In the **Save As** dialog box, type **livepage.htm** in the **File name** box, and then click **Save**. Click **Preview** to preview the newly created page in a browser.

9. Close the open browser window, and switch to Expression Web. On the **File** menu, click **Close Site**.

The site closes, and Expression Web switches to an empty user interface, with no site open.

10. On the **File** menu, click **Open Site**. In the **Open Site** dialog box, type the FTP address of your server-based site, and then click **Open**.

The Remote Web Site Editing Options dialog box opens.

11. Accept the default selection, which is **Edit live Web site now**, and then click **OK**.

The site opens in Expression Web.

12. If there is a default folder for your public files, click it to reveal its contents. Open a page that you want to edit, and then make a change to the open file.

13. Save your page and preview it in a browser.

> **Troubleshooting** The first time you attempt to preview an FTP-based site, you have the option of setting up a custom URL to replace the *ftp://* with *http://* and append a domain name. If you select that option, you can set up the custom URL on the Preview tab of the Site Settings dialog box that opens. The main obstacle to overcome with setting up a custom preview URL in the Site Settings dialog box is the default folder. If your host configures your account to publish into *ftp://{domain}*, it will function properly. If you have to publish into *ftp://{domain}/ {root FTP folder}*, it will not function properly.
>
> If you can't open your FTP-based site through Expression Web's user interface by using the custom URL, then open a browser window and type in the *http://* address of the page you want to view.

You have modified pages in a live site through both the HTTP and the FTP protocols.

 CLOSE your site and any open Internet Explorer windows.

Microsoft Office FrontPage users have had the ability to edit a live site through HTTP for a long time, but the ability in Expression Web to open and modify a live site through FTP is truly revolutionary. It's a capability you will not find in any other HTML editor.

The capabilities of live editing and manipulation are much more robust through the HTTP protocol because of the inherent availability of the FrontPage Server Extensions, but having these capabilities through FTP is also very useful.

Using Site Settings

Whether you have a local site from backing up a server-based site, or a site that you're developing from the start on your local computer, there are some management features available in a less than obvious location: the Site Settings dialog box. By using the Site Settings dialog box, you can customize the workflow and certain default settings for a site on a global basis. You can also do a few things within the dialog box to troubleshoot a site that isn't functioning properly.

In this exercise, you will learn how to use the Site Settings dialog box to make global changes in a site, and you will learn how to troubleshoot some functionality problems of the type that might occur as you work on a site.

USE the *CH10* sample site. This site is located in the *Documents\Microsoft Press\Expression Web SBS\Sample Sites* folder.
OPEN the *CH10* site.

1. On the **Site** menu, click **Site Settings**.

   The Site Settings dialog box opens. The Web Name box on the General tab is where you can change the site name.

   > **Warning** Using the Web Name box is the only way that you should change an Expression Web site name. If you change the name in Windows Explorer, issues might arise with the site's metadata.

The Manage The Web Site Using Hidden Metadata Files check box enables you to selectively use or not use Expression Web's metadata.

> **Warning** This is a feature that you will generally leave enabled. The metadata aids Expression Web in such functions as keeping links maintained, keeping the correct Dynamic Web Template attached to the correct pages, and remembering where the site has been published. If you clear the check box, Expression Web will not only stop using metadata, it will also strip it from the site. Stripping the metadata might be purposely done if you were going to compress the site and send it to another developer or designer who publishes with a third-party FTP client, for example. Best practice for stripping metadata is to publish to another file-based location; in the publishing options, optimize HTML by selecting all options on the Optimize HTML tab, and then open the published site and clear the Manage The Web Site Using Hidden Metadata Files check box on the Site Settings General tab to strip the metadata from the published site.

2. In the **Site Settings** dialog box, click the **Preview** tab.

On the Preview tab, the Preview Using Web Site URL option enables the preview to reflect the URL that the site is opened from. The Use Microsoft ASP.NET Development Server check box is selected by default, and so is its suboption, For Only ASP.NET Web Pages. The Use Microsoft ASP.NET Development Server check box will cause any page to be previewed by using the *ASP.NET Development Server* that comes with Expression Web.

The ASP.NET Development Server will pass any page to the browser during pre-view, but it will run server-side scripting only in ASP.NET's languages. It will not execute *Classic ASP*, PHP, or any other *server-side scripting*.

Here's one example that illustrates why you might want to pass all pages through the Development Server: you're designing a static HTML site, but you're setting your links to the folder that contains the page rather than the page itself. Your links will be to, for example, /about/ rather than /about/default.htm. If you're not using a server when you click a link such as this in browser preview, you will be presented with a Windows Explorer view of the folder, and the browser will not display the default file within that folder. Enabling the ASP.NET Development Server will remedy this situation and pass the default file in a folder to the browser.

3. In the **Site Settings** dialog box, click the **Advanced** tab.

The Default Validation Script Language option enables you to select a default language for *form validation*. Generally, JavaScript should always be selected for this option, because not all browsers can handle *VBScript*.

The Show Hidden Files And Folders check box will change the default behavior of whether Expression Web shows folders beginning with an underscore. For example, if you name a folder *_DontShowMe*, and this option is disabled, the folder will not be visible in any of Expression Web's views, such as the Folder List or the Folders view.

> **Note** The Show Hidden Files And Folders check box can be used for greater func-
> tionality and better management. Here's a scenario: you've built a site, and other
> users are going to update page content. You've used a Dynamic Web Template to
> ensure that the other users don't edit outside the editable regions you've set up. If
> you put the Dynamic Web Template in a hidden folder and clear the Show Hidden
> Files And Folders check box, the users will be much less likely to find the Dynamic
> Web Template and to make unwanted changes to it.

Finally, on the Advanced tab, under Temporary Files, is the Delete Files button. The
button does just that: it deletes temporary files that Expression Web creates behind
the scenes while you're working on a site.

> **Troubleshooting** The Delete Files button should be remembered. If Expression
> Web begins to run into problems while publishing a site, or updating Dynamic Web
> Template–attached pages, the remedy is to use the Delete Files button to delete the
> temporary files, and then click Recalculate Hyperlinks on the Site menu. This opera-
> tion almost always resolves the problem.

4. In the **Site Settings** dialog box, click the **Language** tab.

With the Server Message Language option, you can set the language for the
messages a server passes to the browser. You can change this language only
when you have a server-based site open in Expression Web and the server it's
on is a Windows server with FrontPage Server Extensions.

Default Page Encoding enables you to set the default encoding method of new pages. If you change it, you should also select the Ignore The Keyboard When Deciding The Encoding Of New Pages check box.

5. In the **Site Settings** dialog box, click the **Database** tab.

The Database tab is retained in Expression Web to allow functionality with sites created in FrontPage that use the Database Results Wizard. On this tab, you can Add, Modify, Remove, or Verify database connections to various databases. If used, adding a database this way will create a *global.asa* file and folders that contain files to provide functionality for the Database Results Wizard.

You've explored all the tabs and functionality that are available in the Site Settings dialog box. This dialog box can be used on a local site and it can also be used on a server-based site that is opened through Expression Web.

 BE SURE TO leave the *CH10* site open for use in the next exercise.

Publishing Selectively

From the standpoint of speed during publishing, you might not want to rely on letting Expression Web deduce which pages have changed. For example, if you changed only one file in a site, and you want only that file to be published to the server, you don't have to go through a full publishing operation.

Expression Web provides an easy method for publishing specific files, and provides a method for ensuring that certain files are never published. One reason that you might not want specific files to be published is that if you keep original artwork inside of a local site for management, you don't want the large original files to be published to the server. Another reason is that you might have a *configuration file* in your local site that is different on the server-based site.

In this exercise, you will publish selected files by using File System publishing, and you will also prevent files from being published.

> **Note** You can also use these steps to publish to a server-based Expression Web site.

> **USE** the *CH10* sample site. This site is located in the *Documents\Microsoft Press\Expression Web SBS\Sample Sites* folder.
>
> **OPEN** the *CH10* site if it is not already open.

1. On the **File** menu, click **Publish Site**.

   The Remote Web Site Properties dialog box opens.

2. Click **File System**, and then click **Browse**. In the **New Site Location** dialog box, navigate to the *Documents\Microsoft Press\Expression Web SBS\Sample Sites\ Publish\CH10SelectivePublish* folder, and then click **Open**.

The Remote Web Site Properties dialog box reopens. The Remote Web Site Location box displays the selected folder.

3. Click **OK**.

Expression Web switches to Remote Web Site view.

4. At the bottom of the workspace, click **Folders**.

Expression Web switches to Folders view.

5. Right-click **default.htm**, and then click **Don't Publish**.

A Don't Publish icon is added to the *default.htm* file's representation in Folders view.

6. At the bottom of the workspace, click **Remote Web Site**.

Expression Web switches back to Remote Web Site view. The Don't Publish icon appears on *default.htm*.

7. Click **Publish Web site**. When publishing finishes, click **View your Remote Web site**.

Notice that the default page does not open in a browser, as is the customary behavior, but the site opens in Windows Explorer. The reason for this behavior is that the site lacks a default file (home page) because you set the default file to Don't Publish.

8. Close Windows Explorer, and switch to Expression Web. Right-click **default.htm**, and then click **Don't Publish** again.

The check mark clears from the check box, and the page icon returns to normal.

9. Right-click **default.htm**, and then click **Publish Selected Files**.

Expression Web publishes the *default.htm* page to the remote site.

10. Click **View your Remote Web site**.

The site's default file opens in a browser.

11. Close the browser, and switch to Expression Web.

To make the most of the Don't Publish and Publish Selected Files options, you should be aware that you can select multiple files and then select either of those options. This capability is particularly useful when you have a group of files that you want to selectively publish or set to not be published. For example, you might have a folder in your site that contains files you want only on your local computer. The files might be original artwork, notes you keep about the site, or files that must be different on the local and remote site, such as a configuration file for a shopping cart or other database application.

You've now explored methods for publishing specific files, and also for setting files to never publish. These are very useful methods to use when you're working locally on a site that also exists on a server, and you want to publish only a single file that you've changed, or when you want to make sure that a local file never overwrites a server-based site file, such as a Microsoft Office Access database file (.mdb or .accdb), which often contains more or newer information.

CLOSE any open Windows Explorer or Internet Explorer windows.

BE SURE TO leave the *CH10* site open for use in the next exercise.

Using Subsites

Subsites are an important concept for site management. Expression Web treats subsites as though they were completely independent sites.

One reason that you might want to segregate certain folders in a site as subsites is that you might have a large number of files within those folders, and the files don't change as often as the other files in the root of the site. There's no reason to wait out a long file-comparison cycle during an Expression Web publishing session when you know that the files haven't changed.

Another good reason to use subsites is that you might be developing a replacement site. You can create a subsite on your server-based site, such as *ExpressionWebStepbyStep.com/ new-design/*, and then publish your new design directly into the subsite. That way, you can show it to people by giving them the direct address to it, but the general public wouldn't know it was there and therefore wouldn't see it.

Subsites are a good way to segregate files for architectural reasons and also to provide for greater publishing efficiency.

In this exercise, you will convert a folder to a subsite, publish a subsite, and convert a subsite to a folder.

> **USE** the *CH10* sample site. This site is located in the *Documents\Microsoft Press\Expression Web SBS\Sample Sites* folder.
>
> **OPEN** the *CH10* site if it is not already open.

1. In the **Folder List**, click **SecondSite** to display its contents in the workspace.

   It contains all of the files necessary for a stand-alone site. Imagine that the *SecondSite* folder is a new template or replacement site you are working on within the *CH10* root site.

2. In the **Folder List**, right-click **SecondSite**, and then click **Convert to Web**.

3. In the warning box Expression Web displays, click **Yes**.

   > **Note** This warning box is to inform you of the fact that Expression Web will consider the folder as a completely separate site.

Expression Web converts the folder to a subsite. It now has a different icon, and the workspace displays a notice that Expression Web cannot display the contents of a subsite.

4. In the **Folder List**, double-click **SecondSite** to open it in a new instance of Expression Web.

With the subsite open in Expression Web, you can perform any operation that you could perform on any other Expression Web site, with the added benefit of being able to publish it independently of the parent site that contains it.

There are two ways to publish a subsite. One method is to open a subsite within Expression Web and publish it as you would any other site. The second method is to perform the following actions: with the parent site open, click Publish on the File menu. In the Publishing tab of the Remote Web Site Properties dialog box, select the Include Subsites check box.

Troubleshooting When you publish a subsite by opening it directly in Expression Web, be sure to append the publish location with the name of the subsite. For example, if you publish the parent site to *http://example.com*, but you want to publish a subsite to the server, just append *http://example.com* with */{name of the subsite}*, resulting in a URL such as *http://example.com/subsite*. If you don't append the subsite name, all of the subsite's files will be placed in the root of the parent site. When it publishes a subsite for the first time, Expression Web prompts you that a site does not exist at the location you're trying to publish to and offers to create a site in that location. Click Yes.

5. Close the Expression Web window that contains the subsite. and switch to the Expression Web window that contains the *CH10* sample site.

6. In the **Folder List**, right-click **SecondSite**, and then click **Convert to Folder**.

7. Click **Yes** in the warning dialog box.

The subsite is returned to a conventional folder, and its contents are now displayed in the workspace.

You've now converted a folder to a subsite and a subsite back to a folder within Expression Web. Because Expression Web treats subsites as though they were completely independent sites, subsites can be an advantage for organization and publishing efficiency. Keep in mind, however, that because they're treated as completely independent sites, you can't use an asset such as a Dynamic Web Template across the subsite boundaries.

CLOSE the *CH10* site. If you are not continuing directly to the next chapter, exit Expression Web.

Key Points

- With Expression Web, publishing is the preferred method of creating a backup. Whether you publish from one file system location to another, or from a server-based site to a file system location, Expression Web's publishing operation is the key to success.

- With Expression Web, you can open a site live on the server and edit it as if it were a local site. New features in Expression Web enable you to edit a server-based site by using HTTP or FTP protocols.

- Features in Expression Web's Site Settings dialog box lay the groundwork for setting up an efficient workflow and for managing a site.

- In addition to the Publish Site operation in Expression Web, you can selectively publish individual files or groups of files individually, and you can also set pages to not be published at all.

- Using subsites can greatly aid in overall site management and publishing efficiency. Subsites can segregate files in a logical way and enhance the basic parent/child folder architecture of a site.

Chapter at a Glance

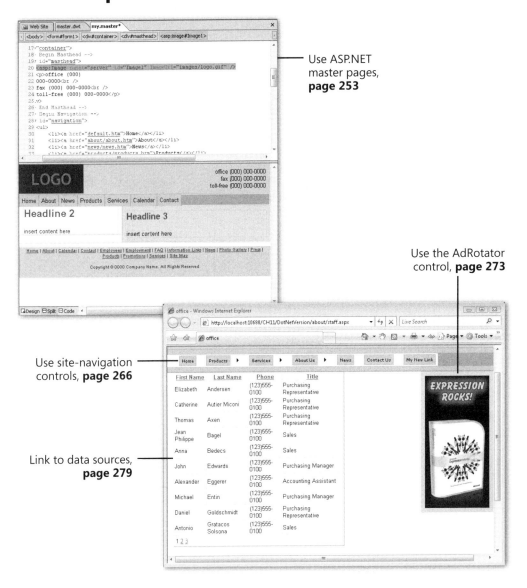

Use ASP.NET master pages, **page 253**

Use the AdRotator control, **page 273**

Use site-navigation controls, **page 266**

Link to data sources, **page 279**

11 Using ASP.NET Features

In this chapter, you will learn to:

✔ Use ASP.NET master pages.

✔ Use site-navigation controls.

✔ Use the AdRotator control.

✔ Link to data sources.

✔ Take it to the next level.

Although Microsoft ASP.NET might be new to some users, it's actually been in use for more than five years. It's a platform that was developed by Microsoft, and it's a huge source of capability. What can you do with ASP.NET? Literally, anything that can be done!

Microsoft Expression Web and ASP.NET make a great combination that enables you to insert some rather advanced controls into your pages without writing any programming code.

To facilitate using ASP.NET within Expression Web, there is a group in the Toolbox task pane that has most of the commonly used ASP.NET controls that are used in Web pages.

One great feature that you can install along with Expression Web is the ASP.NET Development Server. This development server is of particular value, because you can build a site in any folder-based location, and Expression Web will preview that page for you through the built-in server. It's so much more convenient and straight-forward than having to set up a server on your local computer and previewing your pages by browsing them through that server, and it definitely beats having to publish your pages to an external Web server just to preview them.

In addition to providing the Toolbox task pane and the ASP.NET Development Server, Expression Web enables you to modify the properties of ASP.NET controls by using the Tag Properties task pane in much the same way that you can modify cascading style sheet or HTML elements.

For a designer, some of the most attractive controls that Expression Web provides are Master Pages, *Site-Navigation Controls*, and *Data Access Components*.

Expression Web is intended to enable you to work with ASP.NET controls and features; but if you're interested in full-scale ASP.NET programming, you're going to need more than this book and a copy of Expression Web. You'll need Microsoft *Visual Web Developer*, *Microsoft Visual Studio .NET*, or another code editor, and you'll need to learn a whole set of programming skills. You can use books or online resources such as *MSDN* or one of the many sites dedicated to teaching people ASP.NET. You'll find information about these resources at the end of this chapter.

In this chapter, you will learn about some of the ASP.NET capabilities, which of those capabilities are available from within Expression Web, and how to use the most design-related features to assist you in creating Web pages and sites that make use of those features.

Important Before you can use the practice files in this chapter, you need to install them from the book's companion CD to their default location. See "Using the Book's CD" on page xiii for more information.

Troubleshooting Graphics and operating system–related instructions in this book reflect the Windows Vista user interface. If your computer is running Windows XP and you experience trouble following the instructions as written, please refer to the "Information for Readers Running Windows XP" section at the beginning of this book.

Using ASP.NET Master Pages

One of the most useful features in ASP.NET 2.0 for designers is master pages. They're similar to the Dynamic Web Templates that you've learned about in previous chapters; but, unlike Dynamic Web Templates, the master page content is not actually saved to the pages that it's attached to. Instead, the master page content is combined with the pages that it's attached to by the server just before the combined page is passed off to the browser. Therefore, master pages can save a considerable amount of space on your server and allow programmatic access to the template that you just don't have with a Dynamic Web Template. However, when you're ready to publish your site to a public server, you must publish it to a server that has ASP.NET 2.0 at a minimum.

The ASP.NET segment of the Toolbox task pane is divided into the following six groups, each containing controls that you can use in your pages:

- **Standard.** Standard ASP.NET controls such as radio buttons, image controls, content placeholders, and other standard controls that are commonly added to Web pages.

- **Data.** Controls that allow you to easily connect to data sources and to insert data that the controls gather from the data source into a Web page.

- **Validation.** Controls that are designed to enable you to perform validation on your ASP.NET forms.

- **Navigation.** Controls that are designed to enable you to create navigation systems without having to write any programming code.

- **Login.** Controls that are designed to enable you to implement the user interface for membership systems in an ASP.NET site.

- **WebParts.** Controls for creating Web sites that enable end users to modify the content, appearance, and behavior of Web pages directly from a browser.

> **Note** When you're adding ASP.NET controls to your page, it will be much easier if you can see a visual representation of them: To do so, point to Visual Aids on the View menu, and then click Empty Containers and ASP.NET Non-visual Controls.

In this exercise, you will create a master page and then create new pages from the master page.

> **USE** the *CH11* sample site. This site is located in the *Documents\Microsoft Press\Expression Web SBS\Sample Sites* folder.
> **BE SURE TO** start Expression Web before beginning this exercise.
> **OPEN** the *CH11* site.

Note The Web site for Chapter 11 is based on the Small Business 3 template. The *DotNetVersion* folder at the root of the site contains ASP.NET example pages and other files that are necessary for the exercises.

1. Open the *master.dwt* file.

   This is the default Dynamic Web Template for this site.

2. Click the **<body>** arrow on the quick tag selector bar, and then click **Select Tag Contents**. Right-click the highlighted <body> tag contents in the code pane, and then click **Copy**.

   This Dynamic Web Template will be used as a basis for the ASP.NET master page that you will create in the following steps.

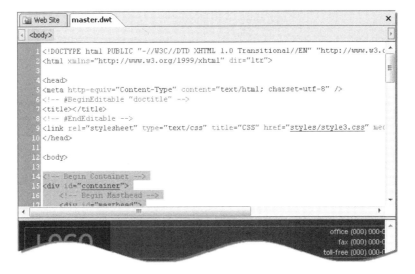

3. On the **File** menu, point to **New**, and then click **Page**.

4. In the **New** dialog box, click **ASP.NET** in the left pane, click **Master Page** in the center pane, and ensure that the **Programming Language** is set to **VB**.

> **Note** Expression Web provides you with three choices for programming language in the New dialog box: VB, C#, and J#. There is very little difference among these languages from a capability perspective. Select the one that you feel most comfortable with. If the master page is to be part of an existing ASP.NET site or application, you should obviously select the programming language that's already being used.

5. In the **New** dialog box, click **OK**.

Expression Web creates a new file named *Untitled_1.master*.

```
    Web Site   master.dwt   Untitled_1.master                              ×
  <body>  <form#form1>
   1 <!DOCTYPE html PUBLIC "-//W3C//DTD XHTML 1.0 Transitional//EN" "http://www.w3.
   2 <%@ Master Language="VB" %>
   3 <html dir="ltr" xmlns="http://www.w3.org/1999/xhtml">
   4
   5 <head runat="server">
   6 <meta http-equiv="Content-Type" content="text/html; charset=utf-8" />
   7 <title>Untitled 1</title>
   8 <asp:ContentPlaceHolder id="head" runat="server">
   9 </asp:ContentPlaceHolder>
  10 </head>
  11
  12 <body>
  13
  14 <form id="form1" runat="server">
  15     <asp:ContentPlaceHolder id="ContentPlaceHolder1" runat="server">
  16     </asp:ContentPlaceHolder>
  17 </form>

  form#form1
```

6. Examine *Untitled_1.master*.

Notice that it's set up with all of the required elements for an ASP.NET master page. It has the VB language declaration above the HEAD element of the page, and there's an ASP.NET FORM element and content placeholder in the BODY element.

> **Note** Because this is an ASP.NET Web page, it requires a FORM element within the BODY element. In fact, if you delete the FORM element, Expression Web will replace it automatically. Notice also that the <form> start tag has the same *runat="server"* attribute that the <head> tag has, which enables the ASP.NET runtime to have access to the form and its contents before the server passes the file to the browser.

> **Note** You can design the ASP.NET master page by using the same method that you used to design your own Dynamic Web Template earlier in this book. Instead of inserting editable regions, you would insert content placeholders, which are available from the Toolbox task pane under the ASP.NET Controls/Standard headings.

7. In the **Design** pane, click **ContentPlaceHolder1**, and then on the quick tag selector bar, click **<asp:contentplaceh...#ContentPlaceH...>**.

8. Right-click the highlighted content in the code pane, click **Paste**, and then click anywhere in the **Design** pane to show the changes in that pane.

9. On the **Format** menu, point to **CSS Styles**, and then click **Manage Style Sheet Links**. In the **Link Style Sheet** dialog box, click **Add**.

In order to differentiate the page you're creating, choose a different style sheet than the *styles/style3.css* that the original Dynamic Web Template was linked to.

10. In the **Select Style Sheet** dialog box, click **style2.css**, and click **OK**. Then click **OK** in the **Link Style Sheet** dialog box.

Notice that the logo image at the top of your template isn't displaying.

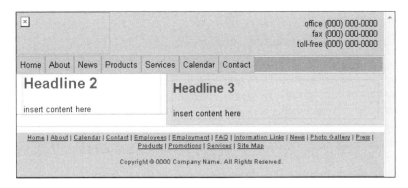

> **Troubleshooting** When you use an image in the HTML code of an ASP.NET master page, you should use the ASP.NET Image control, which is available in the Toolbox task pane. If you use this control, ASP.NET will be able to correctly maintain the path to the image regardless of the folder level of the content page that the master page is attached to.

11. In the **Design** pane, click the image to select it, click the **<img>** arrow on the quick tag selector bar, and then click **Select Tag**.

12. In the **Toolbox** task pane, expand **ASP.NET Controls**, and then expand **Standard**. Double-click **Image** to replace the original image with the ASP.NET Image control.

Your original image is now replaced with an *ASP.NET Image control*.

13. On the toolbar, click **Save** to open the **Save As** dialog box. Save the page at the root folder of the site, with the name **my.master**.

Be sure to save the page in the root folder of this site, and be sure that it has the file extension of .master, which is required for an ASP.NET master page.

14. With the newly inserted ASP.NET Image control selected, in the **Appearance** group of the **Tag Properties** task pane, click **ImageUrl**, and then click the ellipsis (…) button that appears to the right. In the **Select Image** dialog box, browse to the site's *images* folder, click **logo.gif**, and then click **Open**.

The broken image link is now corrected.

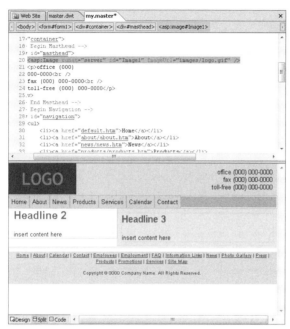

15. In the **Tag Properties** pane, in the **Appearance** group, type **Company Logo** into the **AlternateText** box.

16. In the **Design** pane, click the editable region that contains **Headline** 2, and then click **<DWT:editable>** on the quick tag selector bar. Double-click **ContentPlaceHolder** in the **Toolbox** task pane to replace the Dynamic Web Template's editable region with an ASP.NET content placeholder.

17. Repeat the preceding step on the editable region on the right to also replace that one.

18. In the **Design** pane, click **ContentPlaceHolder1** on the left, type **Main Content Area**, press [Enter] to insert a new paragraph, and then type **Content Goes Here**.

19. Click **ContentPlaceHolder2** on the right, type **Sidebar Area**, press $\boxed{\text{Enter}}$ to insert a new paragraph, and then type **Content Goes Here**.

20. Click **Save** to save the changes you've made so far.

> **Note** These content placeholders work similarly to the Dynamic Web Template that you used in the previous chapters. The content that is within the placeholders in the master page will be written into the pages they're attached to. The content can be replaced within the content page. In a production setting, you could put meaningful text in these content placeholders so that users wouldn't necessarily have to replace the content; but if they chose to do so, the option would be there. For example, if you had a sidebar area that contained a content placeholder, you could insert meaningful text that would be appropriate for any page on the site, such as customer statements, special price deals or announcements. Then, the default text could be replaced on a page-by-page basis or left as is.

21. On the **File** menu, point to **New**, and then click **Create from Master Page** to open the **Select a Master Page** dialog box. Click **Browse**, locate and click **my.master**, click **Open**, and then click **OK** to create a new page named *Untitled_1.aspx*.

22. In the **Design** pane, click **ContentPlaceHolder1 (Master)** on the left to select it. Click the small arrow that appears to its right, and then click **Create Custom Content**.

The content placeholder becomes editable.

23. Replace the text *Content Goes Here.* with **Custom content has been inserted**. Then click the small arrow to the right of the content placeholder.

Notice that the Create Custom Content option has been replaced with Default To Master's Content. This option resets any custom content that's been entered into a content placeholder back to whatever content is in the master page.

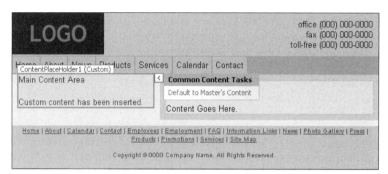

24. Click **Save**. In the **Save As** dialog box, name the page **text.aspx**, and click **Save**.

25. On the toolbar, click **Preview** to preview the page in a browser. The ASP.NET Development Server starts and your page appears in a browser.

The ASP.NET Development Server makes possible a local preview of your page. Notice how it changes the URL of the page from the disk-based location to *http://localhost*, and then appends it with a ***port number***. By passing the page to the browser by means of the Development Server, you are able to preview the combination of the master page and the content page in real time. It's a very helpful feature for developing ASP.NET pages.

> **Troubleshooting** If you have problems previewing pages through the ASP.NET Development Server, you will need to diagnose why it's not working and then take steps to correct the issue. Because it's a development server, it will show you detailed error reports if something goes wrong. Generally, there won't be a problem and common issues can usually be solved by downloading ASP.NET 2.0 redistributable from Microsoft and running the package on your local computer.

> **Note** If you switch to *text.aspx* and look at the Status bar at the bottom of the work area in Expression Web, you will see that the file is approximately 3 KB in size. Look at *my.master*, and you will see that it is approximately 5.5 KB. If these two pages were combined locally, such as with a Dynamic Web Template, you would have a page of approximately 8.5 KB.
>
> The file size of the template is always combined with the file size of the content page. Not so with a master page—the content page is not combined with the master page until the server prepares it to pass to the browser. In the case of a site with hundreds or even thousands of pages, the savings in file size would be significant.

CLOSE any open Internet Explorer windows.

BE SURE TO leave the *CH11* site open for use in the next exercise.

By now, you should be aware of how easily you can keep all the pages in a site uniform by using the master page/content page arrangement, and also aware of how you can save file space on your server by using this ASP.NET 2.0 feature and create your own master page in Expression Web.

Using Site-Navigation Controls

ASP.NET 2.0 comes with three types of site-navigation controls: *Menu Control*, *SiteMapPath Control*, and *TreeView Control*. They can all draw the navigational information from an XML file named *Web.sitemap*, which is saved in the root of your site. The Menu control is the *Dynamic HTML* type of menu that you might be familiar with. When you point to a link that has *child pages* below it, a secondary menu appears. The TreeView control is similar to what you will find at a site such as *msdn.microsoft.com* and is appropriate for organizing very large sites that have lots of *hierarchical information*. The SiteMapPath control provides what you might be familiar with as *breadcrumb* navigation, where it will indicate the page the browser is currently showing and pages in the navigation structure that come before and after it.

Each of these types of site-navigation controls can be inserted into your page from the ASP.NET Controls/Navigation group in the Toolbox task pane.

In this exercise, you will replace the original navigation in the master page that you created in the previous exercise with an ASP.NET navigation control, and you will also add a *node* to the sitemap file so that you can get a feel for editing a sitemap's XML structure.

> **USE** the *CH11* sample site you modified in the previous exercise.
>
> **OPEN** the *CH11* site if it isn't already open, and then display the *my.master* page.

> **Troubleshooting** In order to follow the steps in this exercise, you will need to have completed the preceding exercise, specifically creating the files *my.master* and *test.aspx*.

1. In the **Design** pane, click **Home** in the navigation area at the top of the page. Click the **<div#navigation>** arrow on the quick tag selector bar, and then click **Select Tag Contents** to select all of the contents of this <div> tag.

2. In the **Toolbox** task pane, expand **ASP.NET Controls**, and then expand **Navigation**. Double-click **Menu** to insert an ASP.NET Menu control into the page and to replace the code you selected in step 1.

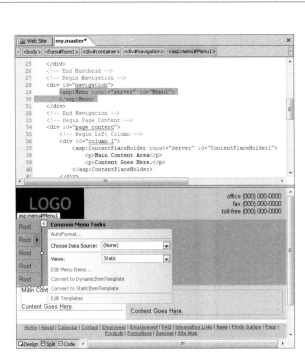

3. In the **Common Menu Tasks** pop-up window, click **AutoFormat**.

The **Auto Format** dialog box opens.

4. Click **Colorful**, and then click **OK**.

5. In the **Common Menu Tasks** pop-up window, in the **Choose Data Source** box, click **New data source**. In the **Data Source Configuration Wizard**, click **Site Map**, and then click **OK**.

6. In the **Tag Properties** task pane, scroll down to the **Behavior** group, and type **2** into the **StaticDisplayLevels** box.

7. Scroll down to the **Layout** group, and click **Horizontal** in the **Orientation** list.

8. Click **Save** to save the changes you made to the master page.

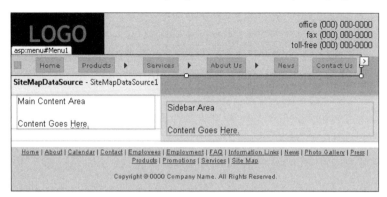

9. In the **Folder List**, click the *text.aspx* page that you made in the previous exercise. Click **Preview** to start the ASP.NET Development Server and preview your page in a browser. Though it's not attractive, pay attention to the functionality of the site-navigation control.

The page that is displayed in the browser has a link on the navigation bar that's formatted differently, and when you point to pages that have child pages below them, a *fly-out menu* appears. All of the visual aspects of this site-navigation control can be modified very easily by using the Tag Properties task pane, and you can change the colors and appearance to match the page template if you want to.

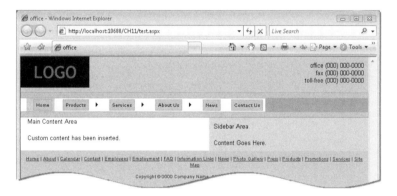

> **Note** The other site-navigation controls can be inserted into a page and modified by using the same workflow. Take some time to experiment with them after you complete this exercise.

10. Close the browser window, and switch to Expression Web.

Because the site map file was already provided for you, the next steps will show you how to create a new page and add it to the site map file.

11. On the **File** menu, point to **New**, and then click **Create from Master Page**. In the **Select a Master Page** dialog box, click **Browse**, click **my.master**, click **Open**, and then click **OK** to create a new page.

12. On the toolbar, click **Save**. In the **Save As** dialog box, name the page **newlink.aspx**, and then click **Save**.

Now you've created a new page, and you're ready to add it to the navigation of your site.

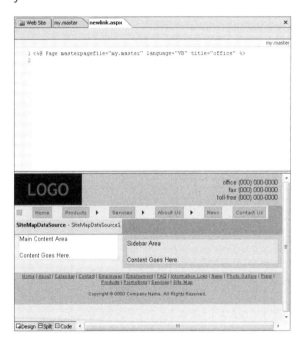

13. In the **Folder List**, double-click the file **Web.sitemap** to open it.

14. Type the following code just above the closing </siteMapNode> tag at the bottom of the page:

```
<siteMapNode url="newlink.aspx" title="My New Link" description="Just
Added" />
```

```
Web Site    my.master    newlink.aspx    Web.sitemap*                        X
1  <?xml version="1.0" encoding="utf-8" ?>
2  <siteMap xmlns="http://schemas.microsoft.com/AspNet/SiteMap-File-1.0" >
3      <siteMapNode url="" title=""  description="">
4          <siteMapNode url="test.aspx" title="Home"  description="Home Page" />
5          <siteMapNode url="DotNetVersion/products/default.aspx" title="Products"
6          <siteMapNode url="DotNetVersion/products/product1.aspx" title="Product 1"
7          <siteMapNode url="DotNetVersion/products/product2.aspx" title="Product 2"
8          <siteMapNode url="DotNetVersion/products/product3.aspx" title="Product 3"
9  </siteMapNode>
10         <siteMapNode url="DotNetVersion/services/default.aspx" title="Services"
11         <siteMapNode url="DotNetVersion/services/service1.aspx" title="Service 1"
12         <siteMapNode url="DotNetVersion/services/service2.aspx" title="Service 2"
13         <siteMapNode url="DotNetVersion/services/service3.aspx" title="Service 3"
14 </siteMapNode>
15         <siteMapNode url="DotNetVersion/about/default.aspx" title="About Us"   des
16         <siteMapNode url="DotNetVersion/about/staff.aspx" title="Our Staff"   desc
17         <siteMapNode url="DotNetVersion/about/leadership.aspx" title="Company Lea
18         <siteMapNode url="DotNetVersion/about/awards.aspx" title="Our Awards"   de
19 </siteMapNode>
20         <siteMapNode url="DotNetVersion/news/default.aspx" title="News"  descript
21         <siteMapNode url="DotNetVersion/contact/default.aspx" title="Contact Us"
22         <siteMapNode url="newlink.aspx" title="My New Link" description="Just Add
23     </siteMapNode>
24 </siteMap>
```

15. Click **Save** to save your change to the site map file. Switch back to the file you created in steps 11 and 12 (*newlink.aspx*), and click **Preview**.

Notice that your new page is now represented on the site-navigation control. Consider that the only file you saved was the *Web.sitemap* file. The addition of this link in the navigation control was done automatically by ASP.NET 2.0 and the ASP.NET Development Server.

CLOSE any open Internet Explorer windows.

BE SURE TO leave the *CH11* site open for use in the next exercise.

Consider this exercise: with nothing but an easily updated XML site map file, a few clicks of the mouse, and a couple of adjustments in the Tag Properties task pane, you've generated an attractive and very usable menu for every page in your site.

Creating this type of menu by other means would have required substantial hand coding of JavaScript or the use of a third-party application to build the menu.

As you use these ASP.NET site-navigation controls, you should experiment with modifying the properties by using the Tag Properties task pane. There are literally limitless combinations of color, action, placement, and orientation that you can achieve by editing the properties of the entire menu or specific levels by using the Tag Properties task pane.

Adding, removing, or modifying pages within the sitemap is done in one XML file. No other pages need to be edited, but the change shows on every page that's attached to the master page that contains the control. These site-navigation controls can open a whole new world to you in your site design workflow.

Using the AdRotator Control

Now that you have had a chance to explore master pages and site-navigation controls, you will learn about another control from the Standard group in the Toolbox task pane: the *AdRotator* control. This control uses the information in an XML file to display advertising banners in a page.

In this case, you will add the banner to the master page in order to ensure that the banner is displayed in all the pages in your site that are attached to it. You will put the banner inside of the ContentPlaceHolder control of the master page so that a user can change it on a page-by-page basis.

In this exercise, you will insert an ASP.NET AdRotator control and modify the XML file that provides the information to display the ads.

USE the *CH11* sample site you modified in the previous exercise.

OPEN the *CH11* site if it isn't already open, and then display the *my.master* page.

1. In the **Design** pane, click **ContentPlaceHolder2** on the right side of the page, click the **<asp:ContentPlaceH...#ContentPlaceH...>** arrow on the quick tag selector bar, and then click **Select Tag Contents**.

2. In the **Toolbox** task pane, expand **ASP.NET Controls**, expand **Standard**, and then double-click **AdRotator** to insert that control where your ContentPlaceHolder control's content was.

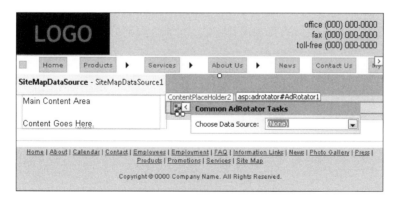

3. In the **Common AdRotator Tasks** pop-up window, click **New data source** in the **Choose Data Source** box. In the **Data Source Configuration Wizard**, click **XML File**, and then click **OK**. In the **Configure Data Source** dialog box, click **Browse** next to the **Data file** box, click **banners.xml**, click **Open**, and then click **OK**.

4. On the toolbar, click **Save** to save the change you made to the master page, click **text.aspx** in the **Folder List**, and then click **Preview** to start the ASP.NET Development Server and preview *text.aspx* in a browser.

5. Click some links on the site-navigation control in your browser view.

Notice that the banner image will change randomly with each page load. Also notice that the area that contains the AdRotator control doesn't look exactly as it should. You'll address that issue in the next few steps.

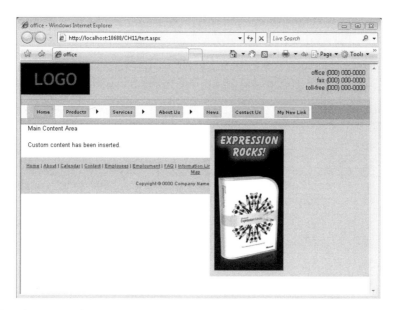

6. Close your browser window, and switch to Expression Web and the master page. In order to fix the presentation of the template, click the **AdRotator** control in the **Design** pane. In the **Tag Properties** task pane, set the **height** to **300px** and the **width** to **150px**.

7. Click **<div#column_r>** on the quick tag selector bar to select the right column. On the **CSS Properties** tab of the **Tag Properties** task pane, set the **height** to **300px** and the **width** to **150px**.

8. Click **ContentPlaceHolder1** in the **Design** pane, and then click **<div#column_l>** on the quick tag selector bar. In the **CSS Properties** task pane, type **100%** in the **width** box, and remove the values from the **margin** box.

9. On the quick tag selector bar, click **<div#page_content>**. In the **CSS Properties** task pane, type **500px** in the **min-height** box.

10. Click **Save** to save your changes to the master page. When prompted, save the changes to the style sheet, accepting the default action of **Overwrite**.

11. Click **text.aspx** in the **Folder List** task pane, and then click **Preview** to preview your changes in a browser.

> **Note** Keep in mind that these changes to the style sheet and layout are in no way final—they are an evolving task. As you build a site, the layout and style sheets will be edited and revised repeatedly in order to perfect the page template.

12. Close your browser window, and switch to Expression Web. In the **Folder List**, double-click **banners.xml** to open it.

You will add another node to the file in order to display the final unused banner image.

13. Insert the following code just before the closing </Advertisements> tag.

> **Note** You don't actually have to type the code. Just copy the last node in the file from the start <Ad> tag to the end </Ad> tag (Expression Web), paste it above the closing </Advertisements> tag, and then replace the instances of "Web" with "Studio". If the nodes become out of alignment from working on the XML file, just right-click the page and click **Reformat XML**.

```
<Ad>

    <ImageUrl>~/images/studio-banner.jpg</ImageUrl>
    <NavigateUrl>http://www.microsoft.com/expression/products/overview.
aspx?key=studio</NavigateUrl>
    <AlternateText>Visit Microsoft's Expression Studio Site</AlternateText>
    <Height>300</Height>
    <Width>150</Width>
    <Keywords>
    </Keywords>
    <Impressions>
    </Impressions>
</Ad>
```

14. On the toolbar, click **Save** to save the changes to the XML file.

15. Click **test.aspx** in the **Folder List**, and then click **Preview** to view the file in a browser. Click **Refresh** on the browser several times to make sure that you see the Expression Studio image.

CLOSE any open Internet Explorer windows.

BE SURE TO leave the *CH11* site open for use in the next exercise.

In the preceding exercise, you were able to insert a dynamic banner rotator into your master page that gets its content data from an XML file. You formatted the control and added a new banner to the XML file by directly editing its contents. The impressive thing is that you were able to insert a control such as this without writing one single line of programming code.

Linking to Data Sources

The ability to draw information from a database and display it on a Web page has previously been a fairly complicated task. Not so with ASP.NET. Because ASP.NET uses *Providers* and has the ability to deal with data natively, you don't need to write any programming code to display data from a database on your Web pages.

ASP.NET can work with Microsoft Office Access databases, *Microsoft SQL Server databases*, XML files, *Microsoft Office Excel files*, and even *Oracle*, *IBM DB2*, and MySQL databases.

In this exercise, you will display information from a Microsoft Office Access database in your Web page.

> **USE** the *CH11* sample site you modified in the previous exercise.
> **OPEN** the *CH11* site if it isn't already open.

1. In the **Folder List** task pane, expand **DotNetVersion**, expand **about**, and then double-click **staff.aspx** to open it for editing. Click **ContentPlaceHolder1** in the **Design** pane, and then click the small arrow button in its upper-right corner. Click **Create Custom Content**, and then click inside **ContentPlaceHolder** in the **Design** pane.

2. Click the **<asp:content#Content1>** arrow on the quick tag selector bar, and then click **Select Tag Contents**.

3. In the **Toolbox** task pane, expand **ASP.NET Controls**, expand **Data**, and then double-click **GridView** to replace the content placeholder's content with an ASP.NET GridView control.

4. In the **Common GridView Tasks** pop-up window, in the **Choose Data Source** box, click **New data source**. In the **Data Source Configuration Wizard**, click **Access Database**, and then click **OK**.

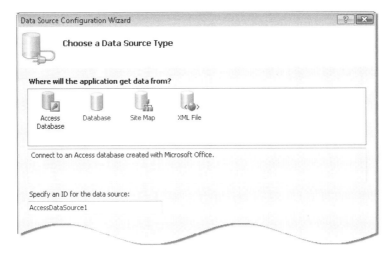

5. In the **Configure Data Source** dialog box, click **Browse**, click **CH11** in the root of the site, and then click **Open**.

6. Click **Next**. This part of the wizard helps you select the data you want to display. In the **Name** box, click **Employees**. In the **Columns** list, select the **LastName**, **FirstName**, **Business_Phone**, and **Job_Title** check boxes.

7. Click **Next**. On the **Test Query** page, click **Test Query** to make sure that you are connecting to the database.

If the query functions properly, you will see a table of the data that you selected in step 6.

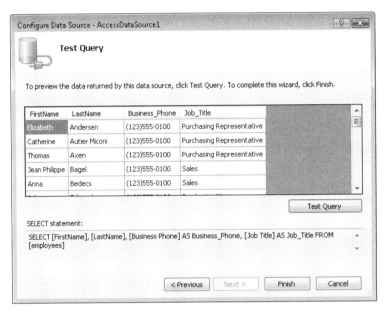

8. Click **Finish** to close the **Configure Data Source Wizard**.

You now have a GridView control in your page.

9. On the toolbar, click **Save**, and then click **Preview** to view the page and its grid view in a browser.

10. Close the browser window, and examine the grid view that you inserted into the page.

Notice that there are now more options on the Common GridView Tasks pop-up window.

11. Click **Edit Columns** to open the **Fields** dialog box.

12. In the **Selected Fields** list, click **Business_Phone**, and then under **BoundField properties**, in the **HeaderText** box, replace *Business_Phone* with **Phone**. Repeat the process to replace *Job_Title* with **Title**, and then click **OK**.

13. In the **Common GridView Tasks** pop-up window, select the **Enable Paging** and the **Enable Sorting** check boxes.

14. With the GridView control still selected, in the **Tag Properties** task pane, type **400px** in the **width** box.

15. On the toolbar, click **Save**, and then click **Preview** to preview the page in a browser.

Notice that the column headers are now hyperlinks that sort the rows below them, in addition to having a space between First Name and Last Name.

 CLOSE the *CH11* site and any open Internet Explorer windows, and then exit Expression Web.

Creating a connection to a database, and then selecting the data you want and writing it into a page was a fairly technical and difficult task in the past. With ASP.NET and Expression Web, you can do all that, and more, without writing a single line of code.

It's more impressive as you dig deeper into the capabilities provided by these data source controls and data views. If you've ever had to write code by hand, you will undoubtedly appreciate the added, advanced features that are available, such as Enable Sorting.

Additional Resources

As this chapter draws to a close, the important point to take away is that there's so much available to you as a designer by using ASP.NET and Expression Web that it isn't possible to show it all in this book. The ASP.NET features alone in Expression Web could literally fill a book twice as long as this.

If you like what you've seen and done in this chapter with ASP.NET, you should continue to explore the features and capabilities by experimenting within the Expression Web interface, participating in newsgroups, reading other books, visiting informational sites, and exploring ASP.NET applications that you can download from the Internet and examine within Expression Web.

This topic provides some information to get started in your endeavor to learn all that's possible with ASP.NET and Expression Web.

Some of the best tutorials can be found at the following locations. Dedicated programmers have spent countless hours putting together great tutorials just to help users who are new to ASP.NET to get a start with the platform.

- *msdn.microsoft.com*

  Microsoft's site dedicated to developers.

- *asp.net*

  The official ASP.NET Web site.

- *www.microsoft.com/expression/*

  The official Expression product studio Web site.

- *asp101.com*

  Great informational site with plenty of ASP.NET samples and tutorials.

- *dotnetspider.com*

  Provides beginner-oriented tutorials for users who are interested in ASP.NET.

Some people learn best by downloading an application, opening it within Expression Web, and experimenting with it. If you'd like to try that method, the following are good applications to get started with:

- *www.microsoft.com/expression/kc/resources.aspx*

  The Design Portfolio Starter Kit and Partner Portal Starter Kit from Microsoft. The Design Portfolio Starter Kit forms the basis of a portfolio application. The Partner Portal Starter Kit is more complex; it forms the basis of a partner portal and uses ASP.NET Login and Calendar controls.

- *comersus.net*

  Comersus .NET Cart is an open source shopping cart application written in ASP.NET 2.0. It runs against an Access database, and if you open it with Expression Web, it will run in the ASP.NET Development Server just as it would on a public Web server.

- *quickstarts.asp.net*

  Provides a good selection of applications that you can download and explore.

Key Points

- Master pages are a good alternative to Dynamic Web Templates.
- ASP.NET site-navigation controls are easy to deploy in Expression Web and are very flexible.
- By using ASP.NET in Expression Web, you can insert a banner rotator without writing any programming code.
- You can easily use Expression Web and ASP.NET 2.0 to write database content into a Web page without writing a single line of programming code.
- The appearance of ASP.NET controls can be easily modified by using the Tag Properties task pane.

Glossary

<a> An HTML anchor tag. When the tag includes an href attribute, it is a typical hyperlink. When it does not include an href attribute, it is a bookmark.

accessible A requirement that users with alternative browsers such as screen readers are able to understand and use a Web page.

ActiveX A set of technologies developed by Microsoft for enabling interactive content with multimedia effects and interactive objects.

AdRotator An ASP.NET control that gets data from an XML file and rotates hyperlinked images in a particular place on an ASP.NET page.

alt tag An attribute of an HTML <img> tag that contains a short text description of the image.

alt text The text contained within the alt attribute of an HTML <img> tag. The text is available to the browser.

architecture In reference to Web site architecture, it is the basic folder structure of a Web site.

ASP Active Server Pages are a discontinued Microsoft technology that was very popular but is being replaced by ASP.NET.

ASP.NET A Microsoft framework for Web development that enables you to implement dynamic Web sites, Web applications, and XML Web services.

ASP.NET Development Server A server that installs with Expression Web to enable users to preview ASP.NET pages and functionality in a browser. With it, users can preview ASP.NET functionality even in files in a folder-based site.

ASP.NET Image control An ASP.NET control that provides programmatic access to image properties.

ASPX The file extension of an ASP.NET forms page; for example, *default.aspx*.

best practices Industry-accepted preferred methodology for performing a specific task or operation.

block quotes An HTML tag (<block> </block>) designed to set a quote apart from adjacent HTML elements.

breadcrumb A navigational aid that shows the page a visitor is currently viewing along with the pages leading to it.

cascading style sheet (CSS) A standard for creating a separation of content and presentation. This technology is useful in Web design for a number of reasons, such as positioning elements for layout purposes, styling text, or applying backgrounds.

cell A component of an HTML table, represented in HTML code by <td> and </td> tags.

child pages Pages below a particular page in the architecture of a Web site.

Classic ASP Legacy Active Server Pages; a technology that has been replaced by ASP.NET.

clip art Prepackaged artwork for computer documents. The artwork originally existed in the form of clip sheets, pages of drawings that graphic designers could cut out and use in compositions.

code hyperlink A special hyperlink visible only in the code view within Expression Web. Pressing Ctrl while clicking the code hyperlink shifts the work area's focus to the CSS style or other source code to which the link refers.

Code Snippets list The list of code, either supplied with Expression Web or user-customized, that resides in the Code Snippet tool in Expression Web.

columns Table cells arranged vertically in relation to each other.

comments An HTML element that a designer can use to make comments in the code of a page. The comments aren't visible when rendered in a browser; for example, `<!-- this is a comment -->`.

configuration file A file that contains certain constants that are used by server-side code or scripting. For example, a configuration file might contain a database connection string, the base URL of certain pages within a site, or certain elements like the site's name.

contact forms A form used to allow a site visitor to enter input for the purpose of initiating contact.

cross-browser compatibility The ability of a Web page or pages to appear similarly in various Web browsers and allow their functionality to be maintained regardless of the browser they are being viewed with.

cross-platform compatibility The ability of an application to function on multiple computer operating systems, such as Windows, UNIX, and Macintosh.

CSS class A cascading style sheet element that can be applied to multiple elements in a Web page. On the style sheet, the class name is always prefixed by a period (.).

CSS ID A cascading style sheet element that can be applied only once to an element in a Web page. On the style sheet, the ID name is always prefixed by a number sign (#).

Data Access Components ASP.NET components that enable interaction with various databases.

database A format for storing and retrieving information. Usually presented as a relational format where information within it contains references to other information within the database.

Database Results Wizard A feature in Microsoft Office FrontPage that enables users to create, read from, write to, and display data from a database.

default file A file on a Web server that is passed to the browser automatically if the browser requests a folder only and not a specific file.

definition list An HTML list similar to the ordered list and bulleted list but designed to contain terms and definitions.

disk-based site A Web site that resides in the folder structure of a user's computer instead of on a Web server.

<div> A block-level HTML tag for a division, often used in conjunction with cascading style sheets to apply formatting to the tag and its contents.

DNS (Domain Name System) The system that points a domain name to the IP address of the Web server where the site resides.

dock Refers to attaching a toolbar, pane, or other user interface element to a specific place within the application's interface.

DOCTYPE A declaration that allows a browser to know what kind of document it is displaying, and establishes what HTML rules are pertinent to its structure.

document title An important part of a Web page that resides in the HEAD element of the source code. The document title is what's visible on the browser frame, in the favorites or bookmark list, and gives search engines an idea of what the page is about.

domain control panel A Web-based tool provided by the registrar to enable the domain owner to make changes, such as to DNS records or ownership information. This term can also refer to facilities provided by a Web site's host that enable the site owners to make changes to their hosting parameters, set up e-mail accounts, or other changes.

domain extensions The domain extension is the .net, .com, or .org segment of the domain name. There are a large number of domain extensions available, such as .tv, .biz, .name, .mobi, and country-specific extensions.

domain name The name that a user would enter into a browser to visit a Web site. The domain name resolves to the appropriate numerical IP address where the site is hosted; for example, the domain name *microsoft.com* will resolve to the servers that host the Microsoft Web sites under the microsoft.com domain.

dynamic HTML (DHTML) An arrangement of HTML, CSS, and JavaScript used to provide functionality within a browser.

dynamic site A site that retrieves and displays information from a database or other mechanism, such as XML data. Pages within a dynamic site may display different information or provide different functionality based on user interaction.

encoding A method to cloak or hide the true character value of data passed between a server and a client.

Expression Studio Refers to the entire suite of Microsoft Expression applications packaged together: Expression Web, Expression Blend, Expression Media, and Expression Design.

Expression Web site A Web site created in or maintained with Expression Web, usually containing metadata to allow Expression Web to provide management capabilities.

Extensible Hypertext Markup Language (XHTML) A markup language similar to HTML but that conforms to the XML syntax. Because XHTML must be more tightly formatted than HTML it is often used in conjunction with automated processing.

Extensible Markup Language (XML) A general-purpose markup language that allows its users to define their own tags.

File Transfer Protocol (FTP) The most commonly used method of copying files from a local folder structure to a Web server.

fly-out menu A sub-menu that appears when you point to a DHTML menu.

font tags Deprecated HTML tags previously used to describe what font, font style, and color that text should be shown with.

footer The bottom element of a Web page, often applied uniformly to all the pages in a site.

form data Any input a user enters into a form that they submit.

form validation A method to ensure that form input meets certain parameters, such as specific fields not being empty or the value entered into a form field having certain characteristics. Form validation can be done by using client-side scripting such as JavaScript or on the server with a server side scripting process.

FrontPage Link Bars A FrontPage feature that inserts a series of links into a page based on how the pages in a FrontPage site are defined in Navigation view.

FrontPage proprietary Technology that requires either FrontPage as an HTML code editor or that requires FrontPage Server Extensions.

FrontPage Server Extensions A software package installed on a server that enables FrontPage to communicate with the Web server and provides additional functionality for Web sites.

FrontPage Shared Borders A FrontPage proprietary method of writing common content into the top, bottom, and/or sides of each page in a group of HTML pages.

FrontPage Substitution A FrontPage proprietary method of changing content based on a variable within an HTML page.

.fwp The file extension for a Personal Web Package.

global elements A page element such as navigation or other elements that are present on all pages.

global.asa A file used in legacy ASP applications. The file extension .asa stands for Active Server Application.

graphical user interface (GUI) A graphical (rather than textual) representation of a computer's user interface.

Graphics Interchange Format (GIF) An image format, with an extension of .gif, limited to 256 colors.

header   The top segment of a page's template. This element is often present and uniform on all pages in a site.

Help cursor   A special cursor that gives the user visual feedback. It generally appears as a pointer with a question mark.

hidden folders   Folders within an Expression Web site that contain metadata enabling Expression Web to manage the site. These folders are always preceded by an underscore (_).

hierarchical information   Information relating to or arranged in a formally ranked order.

hosting   A service providing space, bandwidth, and processing for a Web site.

hosting account   An account from which a user manages one or more domains or Web sites.

HTML Mark Up component   A FrontPage feature that allows HTML markup or other code to be placed into a Web page in a visual way and also protects the code from being changed by any FrontPage processes.

Hypertext Markup Language (HTML)   The standard text formatting language for Web-based documents since 1989.

Hypertext Transfer Protocol (HTTP)   The protocol used when using FrontPage publishing. It's also the most common protocol for browsing the Web.

IBM DB2   An IBM proprietary database technology.

image editor   An application that is used to create or manipulate an image.

image swap   A term used to describe replacing one image for another. Usually used as a visual effect enabled by JavaScript.

imported   Refers to files and/or folders that have been brought into a Web site from an external location.

index file   A file that serves as the default file of a Web site or "home page" file of a folder.

insertion point   A visual indicator as to the location in an application where user input will be placed, the location in a document where users set their mouse pointer and click.

Interactive buttons   A feature built into Expression Web that enables users to insert buttons that respond to user actions and provides a roll-over effect based on JavaScript and background images. The Interactive buttons can be used as hyperlinks or serve as the basis of further JavaScript functionality.

Internet Corporation for Assigned Names and Numbers (ICANN)   A non-profit organization that has assumed the responsibility for IP address space allocation, protocol parameter assignment, DNS management, and root server system management functions.

Internet site   A Web site on the World Wide Web that can be accessed by remote users with a browser and Internet connection.

intranet site   A Web site that exists on a local network and can be accessed by the computers and users connected to that local network.

JavaScript   A scripting language designed to run within the browser of the visitor; also called *client-side scripting*. JavaScript has a wide variety of uses but is most commonly used to provide interactive properties to HTML elements.

JPEG (Joint Photographic Experts Group)   A compression technique for color images. Although it can reduce files sizes to as little as 5 percent of their normal size, detail is lost in the compression.

layout   The arrangement of a Web page's container elements, which provides order and placement for all of the page's content.

<li>   An HTML tag for a list item, appearing within ordered (numbered) lists and unordered (bulleted) lists. Each line in a list is a list item.

link bars   A series of links, usually image-based hyperlinks, which are arranged together to give the visual appearance that each link is part of a larger graphical object.

list item An individual item within an ordered or unordered list. It is always inside of a parent list and uses the <li> and </li> tags.

lists HTML elements that provide a basis to organize information. These include the Ordered List (<ol>) (also referred to as the *numbered list*), the Unordered List (<ul>) (also referred to as the *bulleted list*), and the Definition List (<dl>).

local folder A folder existing on the user's computer, as opposed to a folder on an intranet or the Internet.

local network A network of computers connected only to each other as opposed to computers connected to each other by the Web.

local site The copy of a Web site that exists on your desktop computer's file system instead of on a server.

log file The file that Expression Web creates that contains information about publishing operations for an Expression Web site.

long description (longdesc) An attribute of an HTML <img> tag that provides the user with a URL to a file that describes the image in detail.

maintainability The ability to maintain or level of efficiency in maintaining a Web site's appearance or content.

master page An ASP.NET 2.0 feature that provides for templating of pages.

Menu Control One of the ASP.NET Navigation Controls. This control provides a DHTML-type of menu in vertical or horizontal orientation.

menu group A group of related items within a common menu.

metadata Files that contain information about other files, folders, or groups of files and folders. Strictly defined, it would be data about data.

metafiles The actual files that contain the metadata.

Microsoft Developer Network (MSDN) A site and group of products and services to assist people who develop software within various Microsoft platforms.

Microsoft Office Access A program for visually creating, editing, and maintaining databases.

Microsoft SQL Server databases A database server designed for enterprise-level database performance.

Microsoft Visual Studio .NET A code-editing application designed to enable professional programmers to create programming code in a visual user interface.

MySQL An open-source relational database management system that relies on Structured Query Language for processing the data in the database.

navigation components Components available within FrontPage for page navigation, such as the next/back links and navigation bar. These components must be used in conjunction with a site that has been defined in Navigation view.

Navigation Controls ASP.NET 2.0 features, such as Menu Control, TreeView Control, and SiteMapPath Control, designed to provide navigation elements on Web pages.

Navigation view A view available in the FrontPage user interface that enables users to design the navigational structure of a Web site visually by dragging pages onto the work area. This FrontPage proprietary method of navigation structure design has been deprecated in favor of ASP.NET Navigation Controls.

network share A folder, drive, or drive partition available to computers and users on a local network.

node A segment of XML data that may or may not contain additional segments within it.

Oracle An enterprise-level database system.

ordered list An HTML element that uses the <ol> and </ol> tags to contain the items within the list, which are themselves contained in <li> and </li> tags. This type of list is usually presented as a numbered list.

Page Banners A FrontPage component that can be inserted into a page. It shows the name of the page in either a graphic or text format and must be defined in Navigation view.

PHP A server-side scripting language that can be inserted into the HTML code of a Web page. When a PHP page is accessed, the PHP code is processed by the server the page resides on.

physical size The actual dimensions in height and width of a visual element, particularly the height and width of an image in pixels.

pipe character A keyboard character that looks like a vertical line (|).

port number The port number identifies what type of port a process is using and helps keep processes for overlapping by allowing each to use a specific port. For example, port 80 is used for HTTP traffic, port 21 is used for FTP, and various other applications and devices use other non-standard ports.

proprietary technology A technology that is the possession of a particular entity. Proprietary software technology usually dictates the environment that it can be used in or with.

Providers An ASP.NET module that provides a uniform interface between a service and a data source.

publishing The practice of copying an entire Web site or specific files within a Web site from one location to another.

registrar A company accredited by ICANN to engage in selling, transferring, and registering domain names.

remote Web site The Web site that is being published to. The remote Web site doesn't necessarily have to be server-based. It could be a disk-based site being published into from any other site. The key to what qualifies as a remote Web site is that it is the site to be published into.

Remote Web Site view A view in Expression Web that shows both the local site and the remote site side by side in the main work area. This is the default view when publishing a Web site.

roll-over The action that takes place when users pass their mouse pointers over an element that changes due to their interaction with it.

root folder The folder that contains all the files, other folders, and assets of a Web site.

rows A segment of an HTML table that contains cells along a horizontal axis. It uses the <tr> tag and must be within an HTML table and contain at least one table cell <td> tag.

save time A process that takes place when a file is saved on the user's computer, as opposed to a run-time method that takes place when the page is processed by the server or visitor's browser.

screen readers A special type of browser designed for those with visual impairments. This browser reads the content of a Web page aloud to the visitor.

scripts Code that provides functionality or instructions for the browser to carry out certain actions or processes.

search engines Tools that contain information about Web pages on the Internet. A user can enter a search query and the search engine will return results based on that user's query. Search engines are responsible for the majority of traffic delivered to a typical Web site.

Secure Server Certificate A file installed on a Web server that identifies a Web site and provides for encrypted transfer of data from the server to the browser and vice-versa.

Secure Sockets Layer (SSL) A protocol used to do two things: validate the identity of a Web site and create an encrypted connection for sending and receiving sensitive data.

selector Represents a structure that can be used as a condition, such as a CSS rule, that determines which elements a selector matches in the document. It can also be a flat description of the HTML or XML fragment corresponding to that structure.

semantic markup Elements that are appropriate to content meaning rather than its presentation, such as using HTML tags to describe and order the elements of a Web page based on their meaning rather than their presentation.

server An application or hardware device designed to process Web pages and pass them to browsers.

server logs A file or group of files that a Web server maintains. These files contain a broad range of information about the site, the files within the site, and the visitors who request the files.

server side Actions that take place on the Web server as opposed to locally or within a browser.

server-based site A site that exists within the structure of a Web server and can be accessed through the Internet as opposed to a site that exists within the folder structure of a desktop computer.

server-side scripting Scripting or programming code that must be executed by a Web server as opposed to client-side scripting, which executes in a visitor's browser.

shopping cart An application that runs on a Web server and enables e-commerce so that site visitors can order, pay for, and, in some cases, take delivery digitally of products.

SiteMapPath Control An ASP.NET 2.0 Navigation Control that provides a tree view menu similar to the folders pane navigational arrangement in Windows Explorer.

slice To divide a larger image into multiple pieces. This technique is done in an image editor in order to prepare graphics for use in an HTML layout. The term can also refer to an image that is a segment of a larger image that has been sliced.

standards-compliant HTML code that follows the standards for its document type as established by the World Wide Web Consortium (W3C).

state The condition of a hyperlink or button, such as normal, hovered, active, and visited.

static pages Web pages based on HTML that provide the same information regardless of user interaction.

subsites A division of folders within Expression Web. A subsite is a folder that Expression Web treats as if it were a complete and independent Web site rather than as a subfolder of a larger site.

table-free A layout that doesn't require an HTML table for positioning of elements. The practice of table-based layout is deprecated in favor of CSS layout.

tables An HTML element used in Web pages. This element was originally intended to provide ordering of tabular data but was also used for graphical layout of Web pages, a practice that has been deprecated in favor of using cascading style sheets for layout and tables only for the presentation of data.

tabular Data calculated with or making use of a table; for example, logarithms.

template packages Third-party products that a designer can use to create a Web page or Web site layout. Generally, these packages come with source images and HTML files with the source images used in the layout.

templates A predesigned layout and set of pages from which to create a Web site.

templating system A system used in order to provide uniformity and improve maintainability within a group of pages.

<th> An HTML tag that defines a table header cell. By default, the text in this cell is bold and centered.

themes A FrontPage-proprietary method of applying uniform formatting to a group of pages. This method has been discontinued in favor of cascading style sheets and other technologies.

third-party FTP client An FTP application used to transfer folders and files to or from a Web server.

thumbnail A small image representation usually linked to a larger version.

tiling A term used to describe how a background image repeats over and over until it fills the background of an HTML element.

time stamps A reference in a file or in the metadata for a file denoting when a particular operation occurred; for example, publishing, editing, or creation.

timing out When a publishing operation takes longer than a server is configured to allow, the operation fails and the connection is reset.

tooltip A small text message that pops up when a users points to an element; it usually contains the name of a button or other information about an element.

transparent background The background of a GIF or PNG image that has no color information, and any element under it is visible through the background.

TreeView Control An ASP.NET 2.0 control that renders a folder structure type of navigation element similar to a folder list pane in Windows Explorer and is suited for large numbers of hierarchical pages.

<ul> An HTML tag for an unordered (bulleted) list.

undock To remove a toolbar or pane from a location in the user interface where it was affixed.

unordered list An HTML element used for the creation of a list that doesn't require a specific order. It is most commonly presented as a bulleted list and uses the <ul> and </ul> tags to surround list items.

URL (Uniform Resource Locator) The "friendly name" by which a user can locate a Web site.

user interface (UI) The conduit between a user and a computer program.

Visual Basic Editor A tool used to create, modify, and maintain Microsoft Visual Basic for Applications (VBA) procedures and modules in most Microsoft Office applications.

Visual Basic Scripting Edition (VBScript) Client-side scripting similar to JavaScript but much less common due to the fact that it's not a cross-browser scripting language and therefore can't be used in all browsers.

Visual Web Developer A free application produced by Microsoft designed to help users write programming code in a visual user interface.

watermark A term referring to a Web background that does not move when the page is scrolled; it generally is a low-intensity color, and text appears directly over it.

Web Bots FrontPage proprietary code used in order to provide extended functionality of a Web page.

Web-based Distributed Authoring and Versioning (WebDAV) A publishing method available in Expression Web that is a set of platform-independent extensions enabling users to edit and manage files collaboratively.

Web.sitemap An XML file that ASP.NET 2.0 uses to create the link elements in a Navigation Control.

Windows Explorer A tool built into the Windows operating system that enables you to browse, view, copy, and delete files.

World Wide Web Consortium (W3C) A consortium of organizations, programmers, developers, industry executives, and users that seeks to guide the future development of the Web and ensure that all Web technologies are compatible with one another.

XHTML *See* Extensible Hypertext Markup Language.

XML *See* Extensible Markup Language.

Index

D

About the Author

Chris Leeds is a long-time digital photographer and Web enthusiast who has been a Microsoft Most Valuable Professional (MVP) for Microsoft Office FrontPage for several years. He is also a member of the Microsoft Professional Accountant's Network (MPAN), and a software reviewer on BrightHub (*www.BrightHub.com*).

Chris developed a software product called ContentSeed (*www.ContentSeed.com*) with which users can create Web pages that can be edited and managed by using only a browser.

Chris was a technical reviewer for *FrontPage 2003 (The Missing Manual)*, has developed several tutorials about FrontPage, and hopes to continue helping the user community through the Web site *www.ExpressionWebStepByStep.com*, from which he'll try to answer questions regarding the book and Microsoft Expression Web.

Dedication

I want to thank my wife and daughter for not "refilling my position" during the long hours that I was unavailable to them because I was writing this book. I'd also like to thank my clients who didn't find a replacement for me when I was unavailable to them as well. Last but not least, I'd like to include a special thanks to Kathleen Atkins (Microsoft Press Project Editor), Susie Bayers (OTSI Project Manager), Derek Lakin (Content Master Technical Reviewer), and all the people at Microsoft Press and Online Training Solutions, Inc. who really had more to do with the physical manifestation of this book than I did.

Thank you all!

−Chris Leeds

What do you think of this book?

We want to hear from you!

Do you have a few minutes to participate in a brief online survey?

Microsoft is interested in hearing your feedback so we can continually improve our books and learning resources for you.

To participate in our survey, please visit:

www.microsoft.com/learning/booksurvey/

...and enter this book's ISBN-10 number (appears above barcode on back cover*).
As a thank-you to survey participants in the United States and Canada, each month we'll randomly select five respondents to win one of five $100 gift certificates from a leading online merchant. At the conclusion of the survey, you can enter the drawing by providing your e-mail address, which will be used for prize notification only.

Thanks in advance for your input. Your opinion counts!

* Where to find the ISBN-10 on back cover

ISBN-13: 000-0-0000-0000-0
ISBN-10: 0-0000-0000-0

Example only. Each book has unique ISBN.

Microsoft®
Press

www.microsoft.com/learning/booksurvey/